D1406622

www.wadsworth.com

www.wadsworth.com is the World Wide Web site for Wadsworth and is your direct source to dozens of online resources.

At www.wadsworth.com you can find out about supplements, demonstration software, and student resources. You can also send email to many of our authors and preview new publications and exciting new technologies.

www.wadsworth.com

Changing the way the world learns®

Defending the Homeland

Domestic Intelligence, Law Enforcement, and Security

JONATHAN R. WHITE
Grand Valley State University

THOMSON
WADSWORTH

Australia • Canada • Mexico • Singapore • Spain • United Kingdom • United States

THOMSON
WADSWORTH

Senior Acquisitions Editor, Criminal Justice: Sabra Horne
Assistant Editor: Dawn Mesa
Editorial Assistant: Paul Massicotte
Technology Project Manager: Susan DeVanna
Marketing Manager: Dory Schaeffer
Marketing Assistant: Neena Chandra
Advertising Project Manager: Stacey Purviance
Project Manager, Editorial Production: Megan E. Hansen

Print/Media Buyer: Doreen Suruki
Permissions Editor: Elizabeth Zuber
Production Service: Shepherd, Inc.
Copy Editor: Terry Winsor
Cover Designer: Yvo Riezebos
Cover Image: Dan Holmberg/Photonica
Text and Cover Printer: Transcontinental Printing/Louiseville
Compositor: Shepherd, Inc.

Printed in Canada

2 3 4 5 6 7 07 06 05 04 03

For more information about our products, contact us at:
Thomson Learning Academic Resource Center
1-800-423-0563
For permission to use material from this text, contact us by: **Phone:** 1-800-730-2214
Fax: 1-800-730-2215
Web: http://www.thomsonrights.com

Library of Congress Control Number: 2003107885

ISBN 0-534-62169-4

Wadsworth/Thomson Learning
10 Davis Drive
Belmont, CA 94002-3098
USA

Asia
Thomson Learning
5 Shenton Way #01-01
UIC Building
Singapore 068808

Australia/New Zealand
Thomson Learning
102 Dodds Street
Southbank, Victoria 3006
Australia

Canada
Nelson
1120 Birchmount Road
Toronto, Ontario M1K 5G4
Canada

Europe/Middle East/Africa
Thomson Learning
High Holborn House
50/51 Bedford Row
London WC1R 4LR
United Kingdom

Latin America
Thomson Learning
Seneca, 53
Colonia Polanco
11560 Mexico D.F.
Mexico

Spain/Portugal
Paraninfo
Calle/Magallanes, 25
28015 Madrid, Spain

To Marcia, with love

Table of Contents

Preface

After the tragedies of September 11, 2001, national policymakers called state and local law enforcement agencies to national defense. Unfortunately, the national call came with a confused agenda and no clear directives. Local police chiefs and sheriffs were willing to help, but most of them did not know what to do. Some increased security while others called for more proactive measures. Confused by nebulous missions, national alert systems, and lack of funding, state and local police were confronted with a dilemma. They wanted to defend the homeland, but they did not know exactly what they were supposed to do.

Many law enforcement executives remain confused because the issue of homeland security is evolving. Discussions in democracies are healthy, and some of the confusion is actually a good thing. There are so many critical issues at stake, such as civil liberties, intelligence gathering, privacy rights, police organization and structure, and the relationship between federal and local law enforcement. It is important to discuss issues before we take actions and to keep talking after decisions are made. The purpose of this book is to contribute to the discussion of homeland security, especially as it applies to domestic intelligence, police administration, and security. This short work is designed to raise questions rather than answer them. The purpose is to generate discussion and reflection in collegiate criminal justice and law enforcement circles.

Defending the Homeland is designed to discuss the role of state and local law enforcement in national defense. It is a text for police officers, criminal justice students, and law enforcement policymakers. Designed as a supplemental work for classes in police administration and terrorism, it can also serve as a text for courses in police policy. The purpose of the book is to raise questions about the role of state and local law enforcement in national defense, a role that cannot be defined without a discussion of the issues raised by redefining police functions. This book is an attempt to encourage professional and academic debates about the process of defending America with state and local police agencies.

Americans cannot simply assume that the police have a role in national defense. To begin with, state and local law enforcement agencies are consumed with local politics, budgets, and other localized issues. They seldom have a cosmopolitan world view and leaders are not rewarded for considering international issues. If the police are used to enhance national defense, it will raise a host of issues about functions and civil liberties. In short, incorporating law enforcement in national defense will change the nature of American police work. These issues need to be examined by citizens and elected officials, but they also need to be discussed in college class rooms and police training sessions. This book is aimed at the latter.

This text provides a format for discussing some of the issues involved in homeland security. Chapter 1 begins with an examination of terrorism and its relationship to law enforcement. Chapter 2 introduces issues concerning police power and civil liberties. The problems of changing bureaucratic structures are examined in Chapter 3, and the nature of conflict in the modern world is presented from a law enforcement perspective in Chapter 4. If the public decides to charge law enforcement with homeland defense, the text describes both offensive and defensive strategies in Chapters 5 and 6. Chapter 7 speculates about the future.

TEACHING AND LEARNING AIDS

This book is designed for college classrooms and in-service training, and several teaching and learning aids are included to facilitate critical reflection, discussion, and the mastery of material. These teaching and learning aids include:

- Learning objectives at the beginning of each chapter.

- Sub-headings to match learning objectives.

- CLOSE-UPS to reinforce objectives or prompt discussions and to summarize major issues like the USA Patriot Act and the al Qaeda manual.

- Summaries of emergency plans such as the federal government's CONPLAN and guidelines from the Center for Disease Control and Prevention.

- Examinations of controversial policies.

- Blend of media, professional, and scholarly sources into a general overview for students.

ACKNOWLEDGMENTS

Three colleagues provided review and comments of earlier drafts, and I appreciate their work. I am deeply indebted to D. Douglas Bodrero for his extensive critical review of the first manuscript. His well-founded critique and insight enhanced the final draft. Dr. Robert Taylor provided an excellent conceptual view of the work. His comments redirected my initial efforts and solidified my ideas. Dr. Morris Jenkins provided excellent comments on balancing militaristic tendencies in law enforcement with human service operations. Six other reviewers provided critical insight that focused the final draft. I would like to thank Dr. Harold Becker, Dr. Gardel Fuertado, Dr. Robert McCrie, Dr. Gary Perlstein, Dr. Xin Ren, and Dr. Andrew Waskey. The comments of these people enhanced the strength of the book, and weaknesses or factual errors are mine alone.

I also wish to express my gratitude to colleagues from Grand Valley State University. In December 2001 President Mark Murray allowed me to take a leave from the dean's office to work with the Bureau of Justice Assistance, (BJA) State and Local Anti-Terrorist Training Program. In July 2002 he allowed me to step away from Grand Valley State University for an extended period. I am also grateful to Dean Erika King for taking the reins of the Social Sciences Division.

I am also grateful to my colleagues at the Institute for Intergovernmental Research. Thanks to the SLATT team: Art Van Dorn, Jennifer Turner, Jerry Taylor, Dave Crane, Jim Keathly, Robert Harris, Gary Clyman, Marcie Kilgore, Dr. Randy Borum, Gene Slade, Bill Dyson, Jerry Marynik, and Tracy Pigott. The people who provide foresight and leadership, Emory Williams and Doug Bodrero, also have my heartfelt gratitude.

DISCLAIMER

This book was prepared while working with the Bureau of Justice Assistance, State and Local Anti-Terrorist Training program under a joint grant with the Institute of Intergovernmental Research and the Federal Bureau of Investigation. The content does not necessarily reflect the opinions or policies from any entity of the United States Department of Justice or the Institute for Intergovernmental Research.

1

⟶⟵

Terrorism, Patriotism, and Dilemmas of Law Enforcement

The events of September 11, 2001, changed America; they will have a long-term impact on American policing and the implications and policies resulting from September 11 will not be without controversy. Some people claimed American intelligence failed, while President Bush publicly chastised the Immigration and Naturalization Service (INS). In New Jersey the state police developed a joint intelligence operation with federal law enforcement, while in Seattle, city officials initially ordered local police not to assist the FBI with interviews of Middle Eastern people. In short, there was no standard operating model for law enforcement on September 11 and the role of state and local police agencies varies today. The purpose of this chapter is to introduce the scope of the problem facing American law enforcement, the dilemmas confronting policy, and the background behind controversies involving intelligence policies.

After reading this chapter, you should be able to

1. Summarize some of the intelligence-gathering opportunities state and local law enforcement officers had with the September 11 terrorists prior to the suicide attacks.

2. Describe the impact of September 11 on routine law enforcement roles.

3. Explain organizational hesitations about using state and local law enforcement officers as the "eyes and ears" for national defense intelligence.

4. Summarize the USA Patriot Act.

5. List the types of potential terrorist threats facing American law enforcement.

6. Define the "intelligence dilemma" for state and local law enforcement.

7. Define major concepts surrounding law enforcement's potential role in homeland security.

THE DAY AMERICA'S WORLD CHANGED

When Ziad Jarrah returned to the United Arab Emirates (UAE) from Afghanistan in the fall of 2000, he was under police surveillance. UAE police officers, maintaining routine observation on suspected al Qaeda terrorists, found their attention drawn to Jarrah. Because of his frequent business trips to Pakistan and Afghanistan, Jarrah became an intelligence concern. A shadow war of terrorism lurks throughout the Persian Gulf, and when confronted with suspicious intelligence information, law enforcement officers in the Arabian peninsula are usually quick to take action. Investigators decided to bring Jarrah in for questioning in late January 2001.

After initial questioning, the Lebanese-born suspect appeared to have logical reasons for his frequent visits. Some officers, no doubt, wanted to detain him based on his patterns of travel, but the police did not have enough information to warrant arrest. They let him go with the hope of gaining further evidence. Jarrah had other ideas. Following a pattern common in al Qaeda sleeper cells, Jarrah fled the country as soon as he was released. He skipped to Germany and eventually came to the United States, where he obtained a driver's license listing a Virginia address. UAE intelligence agencies alerted German intelligence, and the Germans alerted their counterparts in the United States. On the evening of September 9, 2001 Jarrah sped down a Maryland interstate highway in a rented car.

Just as darkness fell, the radar sensor in Trooper Joseph Catalano's Maryland State Police cruiser clocked Jarrah's speeding car. A veteran professional, Catalano confirmed the speed, moved behind the vehicle, and pulled Jarrah over. Trooper Catalano had quite a bit of information at his disposal—information that all good police officers utilize when making a stop—but he did not know that American intelligence agencies had received a warning about some type of attack. He was not aware that the intelligence services of two countries were forwarding warnings to the United States about suspicious activities from Osama bin Laden. He had no way of knowing (Biemer, 1-9-02, p. A-6).

A videotape in the state police cruiser gave the details of the stop. The focus was fuzzy, but Catalano could be seen approaching the car and returning with a citation. Jarrah was polite and cooperative. Colonel David Mitchell, commander of the Maryland State Police, would later say, "There were no circumstances to question the gentleman more than we did." Catalano would reiterate his commander's assessment saying there were "no red flags at all. It was a routine traffic stop." Their conclusions were quite correct. There were no systems

---

BOX 1.1   Close-Up: Intelligence in Law Enforcement

State and local officers had contact with the September 11 terrorists prior to the suicide attacks, and intelligence agencies had some level of awareness of their potential threats. Assume that state and local agencies had been given full access to this intelligence information. Think about the following problems:

- How could such information remain secure?
- If the information involved no criminal violations, could the police use it?

- Could the police report noncriminal activities?
- In order to investigate, police need reasonable suspicion to believe a crime has been committed. In order to arrest, police must either witness a crime or have probable cause to believe a crime was committed. Does intelligence information meet either one of these established legal standards?

---

in place to share national intelligence with state and local police. In short, there was no reason to detain Jarrah (Biemer, 1-9-02, p. A-6).

Two weeks later a group of sullen law enforcement intelligence officers sat at a training facility in Spokane, Washington. A command officer from the Washington State Patrol spoke to the group, the frustration in his voice echoing through the training facility. He had been staying at a motel in Portland, Maine, he told the group. Checking out early in the morning of September 11, he believed he might have encountered one of the other hotel guests, Mohammed Atta. Unfortunately, he did not know what Atta looked like or that American intelligence officers had alerted the Federal Bureau of Investigation about Atta's activities. He was a suspected terrorist and the intelligence community was interested in him. Hampered by a variety of laws, internal regulations, and bureaucratic rivalries, the selected federal agents who worked the case were unable to share their concerns with state and local law enforcement. They searched for Atta by themselves.

"If only someone had shared intelligence with me," the Washington state trooper lamented. "I think I saw him." Atta left the hotel for a suicide mission with no reason to fear the presence of a state police intelligence commander.

While Jarrah and Atta prepared to fly hijacked airliners on suicide missions, Ramzi Binalshibh waited in Hamburg, Germany. He had tried to enter the United States, but immigration authorities had enough information to block his attempts. Binalshibh lived in Hamburg as a student while forming a radical group of Salafist students in a Hamburg apartment with his friend Mohammed Atta. The Germans were keeping an eye on him. They alerted the American intelligence community, and Binalshibh could not escape the radar. He applied for flight school in Florida and listed a home address in Virginia, but his attempts to enter the United States were thwarted (Finn and Masters, 11-16-01, p. A39).

After Jarrah and Atta killed thousands of people by flying civilian airliners into buildings, Binalshibh left Germany for Afghanistan. The *New York Times* and the *Washington Post* ran articles speculating that Binalshibh was one of the September 11 hijackers (*New York Times*, 11-27-01; Finn and Masters, 11-16-01, p. A39; *Washington Post*, 11-20-01, p. A12; and Masters, 11-30-01, p. A14). All of the planes had five hijackers except one, and investigative reporters surmised that Binalshibh was the missing twentieth hijacker. American intelligence had similar suspicions but had no way to inform local law enforcement. The police would learn of Binalshibh, however, not from the defense establishment or the Central Intelligence Agency, but through the *Wall Street Journal*. A reporter found tapes of Binalshibh and four other terrorists announcing their intention to commit *istahid*, suicidal martyrdom. The *Journal* shared its information through news stories. For once, state and local law enforcement had an identifiable suspect.

According to terrorism analyst James Stinson (2002), agencies were receiving warnings of terrorist attacks prior to the September 11 suicide flights. French intelligence alerted American officials of al Qaeda operations in the United States. This led to the federal arrest of Zacarias Moussaoui in St. Paul, Minnesota, on August 17, 2001. Later that same month, Egyptian and Pakistani intelligence warned the United States that Osama bin Laden had gone underground (Tyler and MacFarquhar, 6-4-02). He appeared to be planning some type of strike against America. These reports were echoed in the Indian news media. In late August and early September, Stinson says, bin Laden's international operatives were told to return to Afghanistan by September 10. Watch lists of suspected terrorists were circulated to airlines, but law enforcement was out of the loop. If the intelligence community was scrambling in the early hours of September 11, law enforcement agencies went about their business as usual. There seemed to be no reason to do otherwise (see Flynn, 2002).

Routine Patrol on September 11

On the morning of September 11, 2001, law enforcement officers carried out their duties in normal fashion. All across the country local and state police officers pieced together drug raids, murder investigations, barking dogs, lost children, family fights, and a variety of serious and nonserious crimes into a patchwork cops call "routine." Morning shifts went home and day shifts reported for briefings. Many rookies enjoyed Tuesday as the first day of their "weekend" while chiefs and sheriffs prepared for staff meetings and budget reports. Some officers arrived for court testimony. September 11 was just another Tuesday. It was routine.

All of that changed shortly after 8:30 A.M.

The first of two air planes smashed into one of the towers of the World Trade Center in New York City. As news spread through the electronic media the country seemed to come to a halt. Some people believed that a pilot had gone off course and that a terrible tragedy had occurred. Others remembered World War II when a miscalculation on an American bomber sent a B-24 smashing into the Empire State Building. To many people, it seemed like a navigational error. Those who studied terrorism knew better. When the second plane flew into the Trade Center, it confirmed the worst suspicions of counterterrorist specialists. The whole world was watching by the time the towers collapsed.

The plot had been hatched in regions far removed from the United States. To most law enforcement officers, religious concepts like Salafism, Wahhabism, and differing sects in Islam were as foreign as the Ferenga Valley. Uzbekistan, Turkmenistan, and Afghanistan were as alien as quantum physics. Local and state law enforcement were caught unaware and they had little help from allied agencies. At 8:47 deputy sheriffs in San Diego County, California, and patrol officers in Jackson, Michigan, did not realize that they were being thrown onto the front line in a shadow war. As hundreds of New York police officers and firefighters rushed into the burning towers, families of the public service heroes were the first to experience the heartbreak of shadow war. Never in history had America lost firefighters and police officers on such a scale. The families, the New York fire and police departments, and eventually the nation went numb. The United States of America was in a shadow war.

EYES AND EARS?

Although there are more than 600,000 law enforcement officers in the United States and thousands of state and local police departments, their formal role is unclear. In many other countries, the role of the police is codified by law or tradition, but in the United States, law enforcement's role in times of national crisis is not readily defined. Of course, totalitarian governments utilize their police agencies to collect information on political opposition and suppress it, but Western democracies have shied away from such actions, and the United States leads the pack. Historically, the American police have never had a cohesive role in national policy (see Walker, 1977 and Fogelson, 1977).

Other Western democracies have developed more formalized role definitions, especially when national security is threatened. Peter Manning (1977, pp. 111–116) argues that this develops from structural contradictions in American policing. America's police have no occupational mandate, whereas the police in the United Kingdom are formally charged to participate in national defense in times of crisis. The Ontario Provincial Police in Canada revert to military functions when traditional police roles are not sufficient to control emergencies. Police in France and Germany traditionally maintain a more military posture than their American counterparts. Some law enforcement administrators think it would be wise to convert the American police to a more military posture in times of national emergency.

The September 11 tragedies have been described as an intelligence failure, but the issues go deeper than this for policing (Rosenbaum, 6-19-02). The question becomes, what role, if any, should law enforcement play in intelligence gathering? The 600,000 American law enforcement officers could become the eyes and ears of intelligence agencies, the first line in homeland defense. If this is to become the case, intelligence agencies need to develop methods for sharing information, and law enforcement agencies should develop a mind-set that allows police officials to process and act on information (*Law Enforcement News*, 10-15-01). Most street police officers, however,

BOX 1.2   Close-Up: "Eyes and Ears" versus "Crime Response and Prevention"

There are two general schools of thought about the role of the police in intelligence gathering. One position can be summarized as "Eyes and Ears." Advocates of this position believe state and local law enforcement officers should be used as extensions of America's intelligence agencies. They believe the police should collect information and forward it to the appropriate intelligence unit. Extreme proponents of this position would utilize special police units to collect information beyond potential evidence used in criminal investigations. The purpose of such units would be to monitor the activities of political groups that might engage in violence.

Another train of thought can be called traditional crime response and prevention. Adherents to this perspective fear police intelligence-gathering activities will interfere with the police crime fighting and social service missions. They believe intelligence should be gathered by other agencies. Other people have a parallel view, fearing expanded police powers.

After September 11, the difference between these two positions became more than an academic debate. Local,

state, and federal police agencies began to share information at an unprecedented level. State and local agencies expanded training activities in terrorism, and Attorney General John Ashcroft ordered the FBI to create more Joint Terrorism Task Forces (JTTFs). The attorney general also utilized his prosecutors, the United States attorneys who represent the government in the federal court system, creating Anti-Terrorism Task Forces (ATTFs) in all the nation's U.S. attorneys' offices. All the federal efforts were based on the assumption that local, state, and federal agencies would work together. The attorney general also called for a "seamless interface" between law enforcement and defense intelligence.

What do you think? Could intelligence gathering weaken the traditional functions of law enforcement? For the police to operate effectively, they must be involved in the community. How could intelligence gathering inhibit effective community relations? Finally, if the police engage in intelligence gathering, will there be a seamless interface in their relations with each other?

have little incentive to think beyond the immediate need for fresh information, and they cannot picture a role for themselves in national defense (Lindsay and Singer, 5-8-02).

The federal government expanded the intelligence-gathering powers of federal agencies after September 11, and this will inevitably impact state and local law enforcement. The equation is fairly simple. If federal law enforcement agencies are to be included in intelligence gathering, and if all levels of law enforcement are seeking to work more closely, then some of the activities in local police departments will be related to intelligence gathering. A report from the Kennedy School of Government (Kayyem and Howitt, 2001) suggests these procedures and activities be initiated from the "bottom up." That is, they should begin with local jurisdictions. Local jurisdictions, especially in rural areas, complain they do not have the expertise or resources to either prevent terrorism or to respond to it. In the weeks after September 11, Congress seemed to agree, rushing through legislation to respond to terrorism. The USA Patriot Act, as the legislation was popularly called, seemed to favor a "top-down" approach with the federal government leading the way for local police agencies.

THE USA PATRIOT ACT

The Bush administration sponsored legislation in the weeks following September 11 that contains increased responsibilities for law enforcement. The Patriot Act has ten sections or titles outlining new powers for government operations. Title I is designed to enhance domestic security. It creates funding for counterterrorist activities, expands technical support for the FBI, expands electronic intelligence gathering research, and defines presidential authority in response to terrorism. This section of the law also forbids discrimination against Arab and Muslim Americans.

Some of the most controversial aspects of the Patriot Act appear in Title II. The purpose of this section is to improve the government's ability to gather electronic evidence. In other words, it allows police officials expanded authority to monitor communications. It allows intelligence agencies and federal law enforcement to share noncriminal information with each other. In addition, it forces private corporations to share records and data with federal law enforcement departments during investigations and allows the FBI to seize material when it believes national security is in jeopardy. This section also contains a sunset clause, automatically ending the provisions of the Patriot Act unless it is renewed, and it demands congressional oversight.

Other sections of the law impact law enforcement in a variety of ways. Title III empowers federal law enforcement to interact with banking regulators and provides arrest power outside American borders for terrorist financing and money laundering. Title IV increases border patrols and monitoring of foreigners within the United States, while mandating detention of suspected terrorists. Title VII focuses on police information sharing, specifically targeting a nationwide police investigative network known as the Regional Information Sharing System (RISS). Prior to the Patriot Act, RISS was only to be used in criminal investigations.

Supporters of the Patriot Act believe it will increase federal law enforcement's ability to respond to terrorism and create an intelligence conduit among local, state, and federal police agencies. They believe counterterrorism will be strengthened by combining law enforcement and national defense intelligence. Opponents of the law argue it goes too far in attacking civil liberties while expanding police powers. They are especially concerned about sharing noncriminal intelligence during criminal investigations. The most pressing concern centers on the increased power of the government to monitor the activities of its own citizens. These reactions are discussed more fully in the next chapter on civil rights, but the organizational aspects of the Patriot Act need to be considered here.

BOX 1.3   Close-Up: The War on Drugs as an Intelligence Model?

The War on Drugs has produced a national police intelligence-gathering and dissemination system. Combined federal, state, and local law enforcement agencies operate in conjunction with one another to gather intelligence and conduct operations.

Proponents hail this process as a model of sharing resources and intelligence. They point to cooperation among agencies and investigative information-sharing systems as the answer to the intelligence problem (National Drug Intelligence Center, 2002). At the national level, drug intelligence reports are synthesized and disseminated to state and local agencies. On the surface, these multi-jurisdictional efforts seem to be an effective tool in countering drug traffickers.

Opponents have a differing view. Many police administrators believe the systems are not effective and they refuse to participate (Herman, 12-3-01). Other people outside law enforcement look at the intelligence network and claim it to be both a failure and an assault on the Fourth Amendment. Proponents of this position state that the war on drugs is ineffective, and the real loser in the process is civil liberty. Critics feel drug intelligence merely labels certain people or groups without making a dent in drug traffic.

Do you feel one side is correct? If so, why? Can the proponents of multi-jurisdictional task forces claim they are winning the war on drugs? Do critics of drug enforcement have viable, workable alternatives? Do parallels exist for problems with terrorism?

POLICE ORGANIZATION AND THE USA PATRIOT ACT

Kayyem and Howitt (2001) believe national security must be coordinated throughout the country, but methods should be developed to fit jurisdictions. If the federal government designs a "one size fits all" policy to protect the country against terrorism, each jurisdiction will experience weaknesses as it tries to blend its needs with a centrally mandated system. Kayyem, Howitt, and their colleagues urge joint planning among agencies in law enforcement, health (including mental health), emergency services, and private industry on the local level. They believe general plans designed by local officials will serve as a guide during a crisis. Planning is a general response to a local problem, and it is a local responsibility.

There are those who disagree with this approach. Attorney General Ashcroft has aggressively expanded the role of the federal government by creating and expanding terrorist task forces. Secretary of Defense Donald Rumsfeld warns of attacks utilizing weapons of mass destruction and advocates proper centralized preparation (Shenon and Stout, 5-21-02). FBI Director Robert Mueller states that suicide bombing will inevitably come to the United States and the problem may be beyond the scope of local law enforcement (Shenon, 5-21-02).

Many people argue terrorist actions have so much potential destructive power, they demand a centralized federal response.

The debate over centralization and localization will continue, but whether changes come from above or they originate with local jurisdictions, changes in law enforcement are coming. Agencies will have a role in responding to terrorism either locally or federally.

FOREIGN AND DOMESTIC TERRORISM

Harvard political scientist Samuel L. Huntington (1996) argues conflict in the post–Cold War era will be defined as a clash of civilizations. According to Huntington's thesis, nationalism and ideology no longer dominate international relations. Conflict will come, Huntington believes, when competing cultures come into contact with one another and one of the groups feels threatened. At first glance the September 11 terrorist attacks appear as if Christianity and Islam are locked in battle; yet there may be more to the situation. American law enforcement faces the problem of terrorism, and while potential conflict between the Middle East and the West may loom on the horizon, the problem of terrorism stretches beyond the Middle East. Even Islamic governments are faced with the problem of violent religious extremism, and American law enforcement has been forced to respond to militant Christian movements.

Religious terrorism is not the result of the relations among various creeds alone. Peter Berger (1980) argues religious clashes in the modern world develop when new forms of knowledge challenge established traditions. People cope with changes by one of three methods: abandoning tradition, making accommodations, or rejecting new ideas and defending old ones. Militants in any faith tradition can exercise the last option and offer violent resistance to change. Benjamin Barber (1996, p. 34) adds that physical survival is often at stake in these confrontations. It is not simply a clash of civilizations, Barber believes. Modernized nations have accumulated wealth and power while much of the traditional world struggles for survival. These issues are at the base of religious conflict, not part of the belief system of a particular faith.

According to Bruce Hoffman (1998, pp. 45–86), terrorism developed in three distinct phases since the second World War. The first involved anti-colonial violence, while the second phase focused on revolutionary ideological and nationalistic terrorism. This type of terror generally reigned from approximately 1960 to 1985. The third trend in terrorism emerged in the late 1980s and early 1990s as fundamental religious groups held sway of terrorist ideologies. Other movements began using ideology as a surrogate religion. The problem is much greater than a confrontation between Islam and Christianity, and America's law enforcement problems extend beyond the policing of violent Islamic groups.

Religious fundamentalism has changed the nature of terrorism, according to Hoffman (1995). Religious fundamentalists are more violent than their political counterparts, they see death as a sacramental act, and they are not afraid to create massive casualties in the name of their deity or cause. The real danger in this trend is that religious terrorists and their surrogates may use weapons of mass destruction or other devices to cause megadeath. Political terrorists seek political victories. Blinded ideologues, such as religious fanatics, fight for a religious ideal. They do not seek workable, compromising political solutions to problems.

To be sure, some violent strains of Islam present a problem for American law enforcement, but they present problems for Islamic governments, too (see Kepel, 2002). The reason state and local police agencies exhibit growing concern for terrorism and domestic security is that fanatical ideologues present a real threat to communities. These threats do not simply come from militant Muslims, they come from a variety of sources, including Christianity. The 1995 Oklahoma City bombing and the 1998 attempt to set off a bomb at a military base in Texas came from Christian extremists. It is important to briefly discuss the nature of all these threats.

Militant Islamic violence is difficult to understand and it has been sensationalized by America's electronic media. Popular American news programming is dominated by "news analysis" where reporters discuss issues with each other, shout down opposing views, and offer insulting one-line clichés when interviewing decision-makers and those affected by a problem. Unfortunately, this "infotainment-telesector," a term coined by Benjamin Barber (1996, pp. 76–83), is the major source of political information for most Americans. If you spend a few hours watching such programming, you could easily leave believing Islam is a religion breeding hatred and violence. In reality, it breeds about as much hatred as any other religion.

Accordingly, it is necessary for law enforcement to focus on one form of Islam, the militant political strain involved in terrorism. Militant Islam can be summarized as a violent religious movement seeking to place the entire world under Islamic law. This style of Islam has been championed by militant secular intellectuals like Sayyid Qutb and religious scholars such as the Ayatollah Khomeini. Militant lay interpretations of Islam form the basis of al Qaeda's theology, while Khomeini's sophisticated theological writings provide the underpinnings for Iran's Islamicist government and the Shi'ite terrorist group, Hezbollah. St. Andrew's Magnus Ranstorp (1998) argues mainstream forms of Islam will win out over Osama bin Ladin's revolutionary brand of religion because militant theology is weak. Many intelligence analysts believe pragmatism will destroy the more theologically correct arguments from scholars like Khomeini because militant Islam does not meet the social needs of Muslims (Varadarajan, 5-3-02). Yet, militant versions will remain (see Kelsay, 1993 and Shay, 2002).

There are other forms of religious violence apart from militant Islam. Violent Christian religion provides justification for a number of potential terrorist acts. The Christian Identity movement claims Jews are descendents of the devil, nonwhite people evolved from animals, and Caucasians are created in the image of God. Some Identity ministers call for the destruction of Jews and nonwhites (see Barkun, 1997). Freewheeling fundamentalists, a variety of violent Christian interpretations of politics, frequently call for violent resistance to

---

BOX 1.4   Close-Up: The Tokyo Subway Attacks—1995

In the early 1990s Shoko Asahara began drawing young Japanese professionals to a religious compound on Japan's main island. A mystic in search of supreme truth, Asahara preached a strange brand of Buddhism and Hinduism inside a group he called Aum Shinrikyo. He eventually included other faiths in his strange cult, convincing many of his followers he was a messiah.

The world is corrupt, Asahara told his followers, and it must be purified through destruction. Only violent tribulation would allow Asahara's chosen followers to emerge and understand the supreme truth. As a result, Asahara's cultic followers began to develop weapons. They were searching for an instrument to produce megadeath. When an attorney sought to expose the cult, Aum Shinrikyo members killed him along with his family. Asahara disciplined members who threatened to leave and brainwashed others. Finally, the cult produced a weapon for Armageddon, a poison gas called sarin.

Cult members tested the gas by dispersing it from a truck one night.

Unsatisfied with the result, they decided to release it in a confined space. On March 20, 1995 several members of the cult released packets of the gas in subway cars merging at Tokyo's central station. Fortunately, the sarin was not as effective as it could have been. Twelve people died and over 5,000 were injured (see Brackett, 1996).

This incident brings many questions:

- Should the police have been empowered to investigate a religious organization?
- Was the religion destructive by its own nature or did it result from violent extremism?
- Did these terrorists behave according to the model posited by Hoffman?
- Did their actions differ from traditional crime?
- What type of information, if any, should police gather about a group like Aum Shinrikyo before they engage in violence?
- Does religious terrorism pose the same type of threat as political terrorism?

---

federal authority. Nordic Christians and pure Odinists, call upon a pantheon of Norse gods to protect the white race. Creatorists separate themselves from Christian churches all together and call for racial holy war (White, 2003).

There are other violent religious movements in the United States. Cults segregate themselves from the community. They may internalize violence, such as the mass suicide of the Heaven's Gate cult in San Diego, or they may externalize their actions like the Aum Shinrikyo poison gas attack in Tokyo. Other groups may form around a single violent theme. The Nation of Yahweh, an off-shoot of Black Hebrew Israelism, demonized whites and called for their destruction. Certain segments of American-created Islam also demonize whites. Militant Jewish organizations have stood behind terrorism against Arabs or any group threatening Judaism. These issues are not the product of any one religion, but the result of extremist branches of religion calling for violence.

When potential enemies are demonized and degraded, it is often a prescription for violence (see Berlet, 1998).

Single issues may result in such passions that religions or surrogate religions call people to violence. Abortion providers have been subjected to increasing violence since the 1980s. In the past decade clinics have been bombed, buildings set on fire, and clinic workers have been murdered. Violent ecological and animal rights activists have generally limited their activities to the destruction of property, but some have called for interpersonal violence. These single issues take on religious significance. For example, many violent antiabortion extremists justify their actions with Christian scriptures. Violent ecologists use their limited interpretation of ecological responsibility as a surrogate religion.

Most violent extremists are narrow-minded people who seek to forcibly impose their will on others. If Bruce Hoffman's thesis is correct, such terrorists have been acting with a theological imperative during the past few years. While religion is not a matter of national security, religious violence is. Religious terrorists serve a cause with the utmost zeal, not to enrich themselves from the proceeds of criminal activity, but to destroy in the name of a deity. Since they operate outside the law, there is a high probability they will encounter the police. This brings a problem. State and local law enforcement in the United States is designed to counter crime. Agencies have little experience in studying violent religious sects and terrorist ideologies. The dilemma posed by terrorism is that the police may be forced back into the business of gathering intelligence.

THE DILEMMA DEFINED

As you consider the issues associated with the possible expansion of localized intelligence operations, the central dilemma should start to emerge. State and local police collect *criminal* intelligence, not information regarding national security. They collect information when they have reasonable suspicion to believe people are involved in crimes. While some people may argue about the type of criminal intelligence the police gather, no one questions their right to gather information about criminal activity (see Commission on Accreditation for Law Enforcement Agencies, 1990; Walker, 1992; and Radelet and Carter, 2000).

The dilemma emerges because terrorism moves the police into a new intelligence realm. Criminals engage in crime for economic gain or psychological gratification. Terrorists are political actors using crime to strike their enemies. This causes terrorists to encounter the police, but not from the standpoint of traditional criminals. To gather counterterrorist intelligence, the police are forced to collect political information. If state and local law enforcement agencies are included in national defense, they will collect information having no relation to criminal investigations. No matter which position you might support, this is a dilemma for American democracy. The police are not designed to collect political information (Schmitt, 4-29-02).

While lacking a defined role, the police in America have traditionally been associated with crime control. They respond to crime, prevent crime, and

BOX 1.5   Close-Up: Coming to Grips with Concepts

The concept of homeland security began emerging in the Clinton administration and it was pushed to the forefront after September 11. It is a reaction to America's vulnerability to violent individuals, groups, or nations that might attack American interests with technological devices or weapons of mass destruction (WMD). In essence, technology has given small groups the ability to threaten national security. Since this book is designed to foster college classroom discussions about national security and criminal justice, it is important to have a common framework. This Close-Up suggests common definitions for discussions.

Intelligence deals with information analyzed to predict or uncover threats. The term *information* deals with general facts that have not been analyzed like intelligence, but in American law enforcement information and intelligence are often used synonymously. For example, police officers rarely say an informant has given *intelligence*, but intelligence officers would do so frequently. By the same token, when police officers have *information* they often report it as intelligence when talking with colleagues. The easiest way to discern the meaning is to determine whether the information has been analyzed or not.

There are specialized terms associated with intelligence. *Criminal intelligence* refers to analyzed information about crime, while *defense intelligence* examines threats to national security. Criminal intelligence is governed by constitutional rules of evidence, defense intelligence is not. *Intelligence gathering* refers to the process of getting information. Information and intelligence can come from a variety of sources like informants, surveillance, and interviews or it

may develop from something as simple as reading a newspaper. *Counterintelligence* focuses on techniques used to discover or disrupt people trying to gather information about intelligence operations.

Sometimes *terrorism* is a slippery term. Brent Smith, one of criminal justice's foremost scholars on the subject, says it should not be so nebulous, while Alex Schmid, a noted Dutch researcher, provides the most comprehensive definition by giving a typology of many different definitions. This book errs on the side of simplicity. *Terrorism* is violence or threatened violence used against innocent people or symbols to change behavior by producing fear. Many people will disagree with this definition and others may like it. The important thing is to understand that terrorism is socially defined in the United States. It means different things at different times. In terms of discussions in this book, terrorism is a threat to national security beyond the traditional meaning of a military attack.

There are terms government officials tend to use when discussing terrorism and responses to it. Generally, *anti-terrorism* refers to protective measures while *counterterrorism* involves military or police force against a terrorist organization. Many times, like the use of "intelligence" and "information," the terms are used interchangeably. The federal government also uses three terms to describe America's reactions to terrorism. *Interdiction* means eliminating a threat before terrorists can strike. *Crisis management* refers to managing an incident while it is happening, and *consequence management* means restoring normality after the incident. Some people, including governmental decision-makers, think

(*continued*)

BOX 1.5   Continued

we should not make a distinction between crisis and consequence management.

There are a variety of common terms used when discussing response. *First responders*, involve any type of police, fire, or medical personnel who respond to a terrorist act. First responders are usually trained to respond to massive casualties and property damage. *Weapons of mass destruction* include: biological agents (*bioterrorism*), chemical agents (*chemical terrorism*), and nuclear or radiological devices (*nuclear terrorism*). The fertilizer bomb in the 1995 Oklahoma City bombing and the hijacked airplanes of September 11 demonstrate that relatively common features of everyday life can become weapons causing mass destruction. *Cyberterrorism* refers to the use of computers in a terrorist attack or an attack on a computer network. *Critical infrastructure protection* is designed to safeguard support networks of information, transportation, communication, goods, and services.

It is necessary to have a cursory understanding of law enforcement on the federal level to discuss the functions of state and local law enforcement. There are several agencies in the federal government with special agents who have law enforcement powers. The Department of Justice and the Treasury Department have the best known agencies (the Federal Bureau of Investigation; the U.S. Marshals Service; the Bureau of Alcohol, Tobacco, and Firearms; and the Secret Service), but many cabinet level departments also have law enforcement officers. The *attorney general* heads the Department of Justice. *United States attorneys* serve in nearly one hundred districts across the country to prosecute crimes for the attorney general. The FBI is the investigative arm of the Department of Justice, but its investigative power cuts across all other cabinet departments. The FBI is the lead agency for dealing with domestic terrorism. Under Presidents Clinton and Bush it has been increasingly used internationally. The *director of the FBI* reports to the attorney general.

In conjunction with the attorney general, the FBI gets involved in several facets of anti-terrorism and counterterrorism. *Anti-Terrorism Task Forces* (ATTFs) are assigned in most U.S. Attorney districts. Officially, they coordinate training and case preparation in anti-terrorist cases. *Joint Terrorism Task Forces* (JTTFs) combine local, state, and federal police officers in counterterrorist operations, including intelligence gathering. The attorney general created ATTFs after September 11. JTTFs started in Chicago nearly three decades ago when local, state, and federal officers developed a method for working together on terrorist cases.

---

engage in social-maintenance tasks, such as traffic control, inside local communities. Although not a formal role, the preoccupation with responding to and preventing crime has become the *de facto* purpose of American law enforcement. Local communities and states have empowered agencies to keep records to assist them in anticrime efforts, but a bevy of federal, state, and local laws, as well as a number of civil rights groups, have imposed limits on the type of information the police may gather and retain. Any move to include the police in an intelligence-gathering system alters the expectations local communities have about law enforcement. Communities may decide to empower their police agencies to collect intelligence, but it means changing the focus of police work (see Manning, 1977).

There are problems posed by domestic and international terrorism, and the role for state and local law enforcement remains unclear. On the one hand, state and local law enforcement agencies are in a unique position to collect and analyze information from their communities. They can become the eyes and ears of domestic intelligence. On the other hand, when the police have participated in national defense in the past, abuses have taken place. The primary question is, Is there a role in homeland security for state and local police? The secondary questions becomes, Do the police and the public want law enforcement to assume this role (Best, 2001)?

There are no easy answers to these questions.

2

Intelligence Rivalries
and Civil Liberties

R emembering civil disturbances from the Vietnam War era, Chief James
Ahern (1972) concludes that the president of the United States sometimes "speaks" from a patrol car. If his assessment is correct, it would seem
the post–September 11 era of policing is one of the times presidential authority leaves the White House for routine police patrol. The president's decisions
about intelligence gathering will affect local police departments, and this will
raise a host of issues concerning intelligence gathering and civil liberties. In the
previous chapter, you were introduced to the dilemma of law enforcement
intelligence gathering. This chapter will take you deeper into the issue by
examining potential problems involved when national defense policies are
linked with state and local law enforcement issues. If the police become deeply
involved in homeland security, the process will require a new philosophy of
intelligence and law enforcement cooperation and the reinterpreting of existing laws. These issues, in turn, will take place in an environment where new
procedures are defined and refined by court interpretations. Policymakers will
eventually define the law enforcement role in homeland defense, but once it is
established, the interaction with intelligence agencies and courts may well
change the original intentions.

After reading this chapter, you should be able to

1. Define the debate between the intelligence and law enforcement
   communities.

2. Outline the constitutional issues associated with homeland
   security.

3. List the amendments in the Bill of Rights limiting law enforcement powers and summarize the Fourteenth Amendment.

4. Define reasonable suspicion, probable cause, and guilt beyond a reasonable doubt.

5. Describe the implications of the Patriot Act for civil liberties.

6. Discuss practical aspects for and against increasing police intelligence operations.

7. Describe the difference between wiretaps with Title III searches under the Omnibus Crime Act and searches under the Foreign Intelligence Security Act.

8. List arguments for increasing and limiting executive powers under the Constitution.

INTELLIGENCE VERSUS
LAW ENFORCEMENT

On the surface it seems simple: Defense and intelligence communities gather information concerning possible terrorist activities in the United States. The FBI is charged as the lead agency in domestic terrorism, and it has communication links with the defense and intelligence bureaus as well as liaisons with the Department of State, which is the lead agency for international terrorism. The FBI, in turn, is also loosely linked to all of America's law enforcement agencies, and although it does not have electronic communications with many departments, it can contact local administrators. It would seem that intelligence could be readily shared on a need-to-know basis.

Under the surface, however, a complex network of interagency rivalries, laws, security clearance issues, and turf protection reduces the possibility of shared information. There is no system to sift, sanitize, and disseminate information to local law enforcement. For their part, American police executives are fiercely autonomous, and law enforcement agencies and intelligence bureaus rarely trust one another (Swanson, Territo, and Taylor, 2001, pp. 196–197). The process is inefficient, but such decentralization of power is designed to protect democracy.

Two personal encounters symbolize the dilemma about intelligence sharing. The first comes from a colleague of mine who was deeply immersed in the intelligence community. In the past we presented papers together at conferences and arranged discussions on methods to disseminate defense information. We attended both academic conferences and semi-closed military discussions. Despite our mutual respect, my friend could never get over the fact that my background was in law enforcement. He continually chided me for law enforcement's concern with procedures, legalities, and conventions, and he was convinced that American law enforcement was responsible for the failure of defense intelligence.

"You guys will never understand it," he once said to me. "You're too busy looking for bad guys and following the laws. Handle murderers, traffic, and

---

BOX 2.1   Close-Up: Intelligence and Law Enforcement: Two Separate Communities

Most state and local agencies remain outside the intelligence loop. Some of the reasons for this situation are listed below. Which reasons are more important than others? What other reasons would you add to the list?

- Intelligence communities neither trust nor understand the function of law enforcement.
- Discovery in criminal trials may reveal crucial intelligence secrets.
- The police role in national defense is often ignored.
- States have focused on managing the consequences instead of stopping the crisis.

- No system exists to distribute noncriminal intelligence to law enforcement.
- Law enforcement management frequently favors local issues over national issues.
- Rivalries among agencies hamper the flow of information.
- Police and intelligence agencies encourage internal and external secrecy.
- Higher education has failed to instill critical thinking skills in law enforcement officers.
- State and federal laws often prevent police agencies from collecting noncriminal intelligence.

---

jaywalkers!" he chided. He frequently ended each evening by asking me to leave the "real work" to the intelligence community. My friend believes law enforcement, especially the FBI, does not have the ability to grasp international issues. Ironically, no convicted felon hates the FBI more than my colleague.

There is another end of the spectrum. While I was sitting in the Columbia, South Carolina, airport one evening, a man approached me out of the blue. "You were just on TV talking about terrorism, weren't you?" Without waiting for a response, he told me that he was an attorney from the organized-crime division of the Department of Justice. Introducing himself, he began a long diatribe on the shortcomings of counterterrorism.

"You guys don't understand the rules of evidence," he told me. He went on to say, "Folks like you are always concerned with getting information at any cost." This attitude, he intimated, was "ridiculous" because most of the resulting evidence could not be used in court. "What good is FBI evidence, if I can't use it in a prosecution?" he asked. He concluded that defense intelligence was a "waste of time." He was especially critical of the FBI's intelligence operation, claiming it stripped the criminal division of agents producing "usable information." "You can't use the stuff they get," he said, sadly shaking his head. Then he looked at me and exclaimed in his most court-impassioned voice, "You're ruining the FBI."

While these two vignettes represent the most unscientific research one could imagine, they symbolize two polar positions. Law enforcement officers are not completely clear about their role in intelligence gathering, and condescension from intelligence officers does not do much to clarify the matter. On the one hand, my friend from the intelligence community exhibited a healthy disdain for law enforcement. On the other hand, the prosecutor demonstrated a similar feeling about intelligence. In his world, information that could not be used at trial was worthless. Both stories illustrate the very real problems with intelligence gathering: Intelligence agencies collect information that is used to defend the country, and the police collect information for prosecution (Best, 2001).

On a different level, these two encounters represent another tension. The police collect evidence within court-recognized standards for investigations. For example, a police officer can investigate only after the officer has *reasonable suspicion* of a person's involvement with a crime. Arrests are based on a higher standard. An officer must have *probable cause* indicating a specific suspect committed a specific crime. The court convicts only if it believes the suspect is guilty beyond a *reasonable doubt.* Intelligence agencies are not held to investigative standards for evidence. Their job is to gather as much information as possible, evaluate its reliability, and utilize it in national defense. The real difference between intelligence gathering and law enforcement is not based on bureaucratic rivalries about differing missions, but differences based on the constitutional use of government power.

HOMELAND SECURITY: CONSTITUTIONAL ISSUES

Organizational conflict between the intelligence and law enforcement communities is a managerial issue, but it also impacts the Constitution. When police agencies gather information about organizations and people, they do so as an extension of the executive branch of government. Any effort to expand executive power will impact the other branches of government.

The United States Constitution separates the powers of the three branches of government: executive, legislative, and judicial. These powers are separated in the criminal justice system, too, as elected bodies of lawmakers (legislative branch) pass laws, courts (judicial branch) rule on them, and the police (executive branch) enforce them. The constitutional separation of powers will impact every area of homeland security.

A quick overview of constitutional issues illustrates points where homeland defense policies and the Constitution intersect. The main body of the Constitution separates powers and prescribes duties for each branch of government. It reserves powers not explicitly given to the federal government to the states, and through the *posse comitatus*, forbids the use of military power to enforce civilian law. The Bill of Rights also comes into play by protecting free speech and assembly (First Amendment), preventing the government from illegal search and seizure (Fourth Amendment), and preventing self-incrimination (Fifth Amendment). The Sixth Amendment helps to protect these rights by ensuring that suspects have access to an attorney. The most important amendment for law enforcement after the Bill of Rights was added to the Constitution after the Civil War: The Fourteenth Amendment ensures that suspects cannot lose their rights except by the due process of law. The interpretation of the Constitution and its amendments have protected American liberties for more than two centuries.

The Constitution guides America in war and peace as well as in the nebulous times in between. Terrorism represents a new kind of enemy, an enemy who will not strike by hitting military or industrial might. For example, look at the September 11 attacks. America's new adversaries used terrorists trained in military-style camps to attack civilian targets and military forces engaged in peace time activities. As you saw in the last chapter, local police officers encountered many of these attackers prior to September 11, but they had no tools to detain or question them. If state and local police are given powers to take part in homeland security, they will be expected to do so under constitutional constraints (see del Carmen, 1991, pp. 73–176).

National Public Radio (12-6-01) broadcasted a special report focusing on constitutional issues in December 2001, and matters quickly lined up along party lines. Attorney General John Ashcroft called for the right to deport suspected terrorists in secret hearings and Defense Secretary Donald Rumsfeld gave orders to detain accused al Qaeda terrorists without trial. Two of the detainees were American citizens. Critics argued such actions endangered the rights of Americans (NPR, 12-6-01 and Seelye, 6-23-02).

Former Senate Judiciary Committee Chair Patrick Leahy (D-Vermont) said the executive orders coming from the Bush administration were disconcerting. According to Senator Leahy, President Bush's anti-terrorist proposals threatened the system of checks and balances. They gave the executive branch of government too much power. Attorney General John Ashcroft disagreed with Senator Leahy's conclusions. The attorney general argued that the proposed guidelines were solely for the purpose of protecting the country from terrorists. This constitutional theme runs through discussions of homeland security. One group is skeptical of increased executive power, while the other sees it as the logical alternative to protect the country.

At this point, it might be helpful to reconsider the USA Patriot Act. In the last chapter you were asked to examine the organizational aspects of the law. When looking at civil liberties, several other issues come to the forefront. Civil rights attorney Nancy Chang (2001) criticizes the Patriot Act on the basis of democracy. It was rushed through the House and Senate, she says, with no public hearings and no time for public debate. The were no conference or committee reports. Rather than examining security needs, the legislation came in the emotional tide of September 11. The most important aspect, she finds, is the increased ability of the government to look into the affairs of its own citizens. By allowing the government to blur the distinction between defense intelligence and criminal evidence, the Patriot Act tramples on reasonable expectations of privacy.

Others argue the Patriot Act is an unreasonable attack on electronic communication (Electronic Frontiers Foundation, 2001). According to this line of thought, the government overreacted to September 11. Technological societies are open to attack by subnational groups or even deranged individuals, and

---

BOX 2.2   Close-Up: Practical and Constitutional Aspects of Police Intelligence Gathering

President George Bush and Attorney General John Ashcroft responded to the September 11 attacks with a number of directives. Here is a sampling:

- Captured al Qaeda members selected for trial would face military tribunals.
- The FBI was ordered to interview over 5,000 Middle Eastern people living inside the United States.
- State and local officers were asked to assist the FBI with the interviews of Middle Eastern people.
- Several hundred immigrants were detained by the Immigration and Naturalization Service (INS). Their names were not released until a court order forced disclosure.
- The Attorney General expanded the intelligence-gathering capabilities of the FBI.
- The Department of Justice announced it would eavesdrop on attorney-client conversations with suspected terrorists.

Many Americans applauded these measures, while many others feared an infringement on civil liberties. Think about the practical and constitutional aspects of these actions.

Practical Aspects of Justice Department Powers

- Police agencies depend on information. How might these directives affect the flow of information from communities?
- Police departments enforce criminal law. How might these directives affect the police mission?
- Terrorism threatens the United States in several ways. Do these measures focus too narrowly on a single international threat? How would you feel if all people in favor of protecting the environment were interviewed for any knowledge they might have about ecoterrorism?

Constitutional Aspects of Justice Department Powers

- Police interviews are based on reasonable suspicion. Did the order to interview Middle Eastern males violate constitutional guidelines for police interviews?
- Individuals have a right to privacy. Did the actions of the federal government violate this right?
- As interpreted by employment and civil rights laws, organizations are not allowed to discriminate against people on the basis of race, religion, or national origin. Did the federal government violate this principle in the wake of September 11?

---

protection requires thoughtful, reflective analysis and reaction. Instead, Congress rushed legislation amending fifteen different statutes. The law gives federal law enforcement the right to monitor Internet searches and to keep tabs on individual queries. The government is allowed to contact roving wiretaps without probable cause in the hope of obtaining information. For many, the provision in Title II forcing Internet service providers to give information to federal law enforcement agencies is not acceptable.

Yet not everyone believes the Patriot Act represents an attack on individual rights. For example, two senators with strong civil liberties records think criticism of the USA Patriot Act is premature (Straub, 5-1-02). Senator Dianne Feinstein (D-California) believes we cannot rush to judgment. Time will tell how it is utilized in the real world, she states. It may be necessary to revisit the law, but first we need to see how it is implemented. Senator Charles Schuman (D-New York) states the law is balanced. It limits personal freedom while reasonably enhancing security. Both senators believe it is necessary to balance civil liberties with social protection.

Championed by the Bush administration, the Patriot Act is a lightning rod in the debate pitting national security against civil liberties. Technological societies are vulnerable to technological attack, regardless of ideology. Whether this involves individuals engaged in a killing spree, criminal gangs, or terrorist conspiracies, a technological society is open to attack. The more sophisticated the attackers become, the greater the chances are for multiple deaths. September 11 exacerbated the issue, but America was vulnerable prior to the hijackings and it remains vulnerable today. Supporters claim the Patriot Act and other governmental actions are necessary for security. Critics believe security cannot come at the unreasonable expense of civil liberties. This debate continues and the courts have yet to rule on the issues.

A PRACTICAL ARGUMENT
FOR INTELLIGENCE OPERATIONS

There were many indications that the United States might be attacked in the decade prior to September 11. German intelligence sources signaled a warning prior to the first World Trade Center bombing in 1993. Progressive strikes by al Qaeda indicated that the lethality of terrorism was increasing. The judge who sentenced the first Trade Center bombers of 1993 stated that he was disturbed by the amount of hatred he saw in the suspects. Information seized in 1993 was ignored for a year because the prosecutors and investigators could not translate Arabic. When original notes finally were translated, they revealed further terrorist plots. Steven Emerson (2002) uncovered networks of jihadist organizations operating in the United States; he points to fund-raising visits by Abdullah Azzam, the cleric who inspired Osama bin Laden to form al Qaeda. Even arrest records in New York, Boston, and Chicago could have provided valuable information on terrorist sleeper cells. Instead, state and local law enforcement unconsciously ignored the information it collected as intelligence agencies dichotomized national security intelligence and information used in criminal investigations.

Domestic terrorism was another matter. Information about domestic groups began appearing in state and local agencies after the bombing of the Alfred P. Murrah Federal Building in Oklahoma City in April 1995. Although the Christian patriot movement had been operating since the early 1980s, all of American law enforcement seemed to stand up and take notice after Oklahoma

City. Other agencies realized that cults, gangs, and criminal groups demanded increased intelligence activities and a willingness to share information among law enforcement departments. The 1993 Branch Davidian standoff in Waco, Texas reinforced this notion, while a massacre of high school students and one teacher at Columbine High School in Littleton, Colorado, also brought a call to action. Some agencies began to focus on indicators in the communities that would show that a religious cult was active or that school violence was likely to take place. If such indicators could be developed and monitored, law enforcement might have the chance to stop an event before it happened. This idea was hardly innovative. It was a combination of good police work, applying information gathered in community policing, and sharing information. The same logic did not apply to terrorism.

The issue of Weapons of Mass Destruction (WMD) illustrates the point. After the incidents at Waco, Oklahoma City, and Columbine, some policymakers began to think that international terrorists could wreak more havoc than their domestic counterparts. This seemed to be especially true in the realm of chemical, biological, and nuclear weapons. Fire departments and state emergency service agencies received millions of dollars in federal aid to prepare for the worst. By 1996 the groups were up and running. Preparations focused on response. Fire departments developed plans for sealing off contaminated areas while hospitals dealt with treatment. The decline in the medical infrastructure became evident as health administrators realized they had few resources for dealing with biological terrorism. This realization brought more money. Everything seemed to be aimed at responding to a WMD incident and bringing the situation under control.

While these preparations were taking place, very little attention was focused on another possible solution. If law enforcement intelligence capabilities were increased; if cooperation among law enforcement agencies increased; if law enforcement agencies developed systems to share information; if national intelligence agencies could establish secure links with law enforcement agencies; if law enforcement's role in national defense was recognized; it might be possible to strike at organizations that would use WMD *prior to* their employment. Such an approach would require a shift in the way Americans viewed police officers and the way police officers viewed their jobs (see *Law Enforcement News,* 10-15-01 and Riordan and Zegart, 7-5-02).

A PRACTICAL ARGUMENT AGAINST
INTELLIGENCE OPERATIONS

When looking at the victims of September 11, arguments against any defensive measures seem to shrink to absurdity. Yet, when the heat of the moment is over, long-term issues arise from reactions to an immediate problem. The first issue in intelligence gathering focuses not so much on the police but on the sheer

volume of information. Senator Robert Graham (D-Florida) was especially critical of both the CIA and the FBI prior to beginning hearings about intelligence
gathering. He blamed George Tenet of the CIA and the FBI's Robert Mueller
for failing to gather, analyze, and share information (Cloud, 4-15-02). Regardless,
when all bureaucratic rivalries are considered as well as the inadequacy of human
intelligence systems, the simple fact is there is too much information. Information is useless unless it is analyzed, and if the police add to the volume of information without evaluating it, their efforts will be in vain. The key to intelligence
is gathering information and organizing it. Information is not valuable unless
agencies know what it means (Thornburgh, 6-29-02).

There are other issues. Conservatives and law enforcement executives have
expressed concerns about involving state and local police agencies in federal
issues. For example, in early 2002, the Department of Justice suggested that
local police agencies could assist the INS in tracking down illegal immigrants.
Conservatives argued that this blurred the lines of federalism and states rights.
If local police became involved in federal law enforcement, conservatives
argued, they would eventually move to other areas of federal law. Do Americans want state and local police to enforce disability or environmental laws? the
conservatives asked. This is far beyond the constitutional scope of the police.
Law enforcement administrators were concerned with the federal request for
another reason: By enforcing immigration laws, local police officers would
erode their base of information. Law enforcement can only operate against
crime when people are willing to share information. If immigrants feel local
officers are investigating them at each contact, they will be reluctant to report
crime or turn to the police for help.

Civil libertarians and others believe the police have a right to collect information related to crimes. When law enforcement has reasonable suspicion to
believe an investigation is warranted, criminal intelligence may be gathered. The
rub comes with national defense intelligence, and a recent case with surveillance
cameras in Washington, D.C., demonstrates the point (Clymer, 6-19-02).

Prior to the 2002 Fourth of July celebrations, city officials in Washington, D.C.,
examined the possibility of combining the district's television monitoring
cameras with surveillance systems in the district's school and subway systems.
It would expand the Metropolitan Police Department's ability to observe
and respond to potential problems. Some citizens were willing to embrace the
concept not only for public safety, but for narcotics enforcement and protection from terrorism as well. This drew the attention of critics. No doubt surveillance capabilities would be expanded, but should all citizens fall under the
electric eye? One city official said the television system was a means of spying
on average people every time they went outside or stood at their own window
(Clymer, 6-19-02).

Finally, relatively recent experiences with police intelligence gathering is
not full of pleasant memories. When civil libertarians point to concerns about
police intelligence activities, they are not dealing with abstract concepts. For
example, the FBI's Counterintelligence Program (COINTELPRO) operated
from 1956 to 1971. Often working in conjunction with state and local intelli-

---

BOX 2.3   Close-Up: COINTELPRO

COINTELPRO is the acronym for the FBI's domestic counterintelligence program that operated from 1956 to 1971. Originating in the effort to target foreign intelligence agencies during the Cold War, COINTELPRO evolved to target dissident political organizations. Issues came to light when an NBC report raised questions about the program and Senator Frank Church opened a Senate investigation of FBI operations. Critics maintain the FBI ran disinformation campaigns against American citizens like Martin Luther King, Jr. in the name of anticommunism. Defenders argued that the FBI had the right to defend America against subversive threats. Most people felt the FBI's program violated basic constitutional rights and COINTELPRO was dissolved in 1971.

SOURCE: *http://www.derechos.net/paulwolf/cointelpro/cointel.htm*

---

gence units, the FBI spied on American citizens engaged in political activities. Many COINTELPRO operations went beyond spying as agents planted false information and rumors about political leaders. In a more recent example, the American Civil Liberties Union (ACLU) charged the Denver Police Department with spying on citizens engaged in unpopular political activities. Terrorists may be associated with unpopular political causes, but most of the people with extreme political views are not terrorists. Civil libertarians argue the police begin by gathering information on violent activity, but quickly move to monitoring nonviolent political opposition. They believe abuses like these must be stopped (see Best, 12-3-01; Levitt, 1-28-02; Wilgoren, 6-19-02; Becker, 7-14-02).

A sense of urgency contributes to the debate. If COINTELPRO was not an abstraction, neither were the victims of September 11. In keeping with the sense of urgency, Secretary Tom Ridge, President Bush's director for Homeland Security, asked Congress to exempt a proposed cabinet level agency from normative safeguards. The nature of counterterrorism, Secretary Ridge said, called for increased secrecy and powers for law enforcement. Former CIA general counsel Jeffrey Smith supported Ridge, calling for an elite domestic security unit similar to the United Kingdom's MI 5. By removing law enforcement from intelligence gathering and surveillance, he believed concerns about civil liberties could be alleviated. Critics maintain this to be a wolf in sheep's clothing. Any domestic spy organization threatens civil liberties (Mitchell and Hulse, 6-27-02).

The practical arguments for and against intelligence operations raise another constitutional issue. The balance of powers principle in the Constitution maintains that governmental authority is to be shared by the executive, legislative, and judicial practices. Quite apart from the practical aspects of police intelligence gathering, the idea of increasing police power may swing the balance to the executive branch. Since we have examined some of the practical concerns, it necessary is to augment the discussion with issues involved with increasing executive authority.

INCREASING EXECUTIVE POWERS
UNDER THE CONSTITUTION

Several constitutional scholars have examined the issue of increasing executive powers to combat terrorism. Professor Lewis Katz (11-24-01) believed in limited government prior to September 11, but he rethought his position in the wake of the attacks. His concerns center on diminishing American rights, and he finds an analogy in drug enforcement. America launched its war on drugs and soon discovered it could not thwart drug traffickers under constitutional rules of evidence. As a result, police power has been growing since 1971, Katz argues, and citizen protection under the Fourth Amendment has been decreasing.

While leery of government, Katz says the real test of the Fourth Amendment is reasonableness. In normal times, police officers can be held to a higher standard of behavior than in times of emergency. September 11 constituted an emergency. It was not unreasonable to interview Middle Eastern immigrants, Katz concludes, nor was it unreasonable to increase electronic-surveillance powers. A long-time opponent of a national identification system, Katz says such a system would not be unconstitutional, provided citizens were not ordered to produce identification without reasonable suspicion. Actions taken to prevent another September 11, he argues, do not violate the Fourth Amendment when they are reasonable.

Katz does believe some government actions are unreasonable. Eavesdropping on attorney-client conversations, for example, violates the Sixth Amendment, a suspect's right to counsel. Military tribunals deny the presumption of innocence. He argues that we cannot sacrifice the very liberties we are fighting to preserve. Katz's argument indicates that the balance of power is a dynamic entity vacillating according to circumstances. In other words, there is no blanket policy of reasonableness, and care must be taken to balance security with civil liberties.

Professor Sherry Colb (10-10-01) of Rutgers University's School of Law also applies a doctrine of reasonableness. Examining the issue of racial profiling, Colb concedes that the American police are facing a new enemy. Racial profiling has not helped the police control drugs, she argues, and it violates the due process clause of the Fourteenth Amendment. Yet, the scope of September 11 calls previous assumptions about profiling into question. As police agencies assemble profiles of terrorists, one of the characteristics may be race.

Colb believes any profiling system, including one having race as a factor, will yield many more false stops than apprehensions. The reason is that there are only a small number of terrorists in any group regardless of their profile. The population of people matching the profile is greater than the population of terrorists in the profile group. By the same token, a number of terrorists may fall within a particular ethnic group and the urgency of September 11 may require action. If a terrorist profile develops and it includes race as one of the characteristics, Professor Colb suggests, some opponents of racial profiling may find they endorse it for counterterrorism.

The Bush administration moved quickly in the wake of September 11 (Van Natta, 3-30-02). Wanting to do everything possible to catch terrorists, the Department of Justice scrapped the restrictions it placed on agents after COIN-TELPRO. Issuing new guidelines, it freed the FBI from the requirement to rely on reasonable suspicion before launching an inquiry. Unless the courts rule otherwise or legislative bodies intervene, agents are free to search for indicators of illegal activity in open-source information, including the Internet. They can monitor chat rooms or engage in data mining. Agents can go undercover in political or religious organizations to search for threats to security. No longer required to seek centralized approval, local FBI offices would be empowered to launch inquiries based on their own information and initiative.

New guidelines, executive orders, and military tribunals have created strange twists in the criminal justice system. Reporter Katherine Seelye (6-23-02) examines the summer of 2002 when two foreign-born terrorist suspects were arrested based on probable cause and sent to trial. At the same time, two American citizens, Yasser Esam Hawdi and Jose Padilla, were held by military force without representation. Hawdi was fighting for al Qaeda when captured in Afghanistan in November 2001, and Padilla was arrested on May 8, 2002 for his alleged involvement in a plot to detonate a dirty nuclear bomb in the United States. Hawdi and Padilla, who would have been criminally charged prior to September 11, were detained much like prisoners of war, while two alleged terrorists arrested on American soil were afforded the rights of criminal suspects.

Ruth Wedgwood (6-14-02, A12), a former federal prosecutor who teaches law at Yale and Johns Hopkins, offers an explanation of the irony between Americans being detained militarily and foreigners being held under civilian arrest. She says al Qaeda attacked civilian targets, gaining an advantage in the American criminal justice system. Al Qaeda, Wedgwood says, has learned it is best to recruit American citizens for operations because citizens are not subject to arbitrary arrest. Pointing to Jose Padilla, Wedgwood states that his arrest represents a conundrum between reconciling public safety and the law. The issues surface in the difference between intelligence operations and law enforcement administration. In short, she says, going to trial means exposing intelligence sources for the sake of a criminal conviction.

Wedgwood presents the logic of the two situations. Common sense dictates that the detention of terrorists does not follow the pattern of criminal arrests. Terrorists are detained because no writ, no law, and no court order will stop them from attacking. They must be physically restrained, Wedgwood says. The purpose of detention, she argues, is not to engage in excessive punishment, but to keep terrorists from returning to society. She admits that the situation presents a nation ruled by law with a public dilemma.

Wedgwood argues that indefinite detention by executive order is not the most suitable alternative. Terrorists could be given a military hearing to determine if they continue to represent a threat. A panel of judges might rule on the danger of releasing suspected terrorists from custody. The Constitution is not a suicide pact, she says, citing a famous court decision. Common sense demands a reasonable solution to the apparent dichotomy between freedom and security.

E. V. Konotorovich (6-18-02, p. A16) is not as concerned about executive orders as Wedgwood. The stakes are so high, he argues, that the United States must make all reasonable efforts to stop the next attack. Torture is out of the question in the United States, but drugs are a viable alternative. Police are allowed to do body cavity searches for contraband in prison, Konotorovich argues, and the September 11 attacks make such searches pale in the face of massive terrorism. Drugs should not be used for prosecution, he says, but they are acceptable for gaining information. The threat is real, and legal arguments against obtaining information are illusory. When al Qaeda has captured Americans, they have been quickly executed. Konotorovich believes Americans must take decisive actions against such terrorists.

LIMITING EXECUTIVE POWERS
UNDER THE CONSTITUTION

Professor Susan Herman (12-3-01) of Brooklyn Law School vehemently urges a different approach to anti-terrorism, believing the Patriot Act to be a law that throws the balance of powers principle out of kilter. She asserts that Congress has relinquished its power to the presidency, and it failed to provide any room for judicial review. Congress, Herman argues, has chosen to fight terrorism by providing funding to the Bush administration, while simultaneously giving up its powers for control. Proposals coming from the administration complement congressional actions by increasing the executive power to take actions without judicial review. For Herman, the beginnings of the "war on terrorism" translates to a "war on the balance of powers."

Professor Herman's argument is based in constitutional law. She compares the USA Patriot Act with two previous sweeping pieces of legislation, the 1968 Crime Control and Safe Streets Act, and the 1978 Foreign Intelligence Surveillance Act (FISA). Both laws provide guidelines for domestic surveillance. Title III of the Safe Streets Act mandates judicial review of police surveillance. Under Title III, criminal evidence cannot be gathered without prior approval from a federal court, and while a judge reviews a request for surveillance in secrecy, the police must prove wiretaps or other means of electronic eavesdropping will lead to probable cause. FISA surveillance differs from Title III warrants. Under FISA, various forms of eavesdropping can be used to gather intelligence. A special judicial review is required before surveillance can be initiated, and any evidence gathered during the investigation cannot be used in a criminal prosecution.

The constitutional concern voiced by Herman partially focuses on judicial review. The courts have not been as vigilant in protecting individual rights during intelligence cases as they are in criminal trials. For example, she cites the record of FISA surveillance requests. Between 1978 and 2001 federal law enforcement officers applied for 4,275 FISA warrants. They were all granted. In fairness to the judicial reviewers, you should remember that evidence

---

BOX 2.4   Close-Up: Too Much Emphasis on September 11?

Notice how many of the constitutional arguments center on September 11. Think about the following questions:

- Do domestic threats warrant enhanced police intelligence gathering? Do security threats only apply to foreign threats?
- After the 1995 Oklahoma City bombing, the government increased law enforcement powers, and the same thing happened after September 11. Is the federal government spending too much time reacting to particular problems?
- Are Americans caught in the mood of the moment? That is, do we react to our immediate problems and tend to forget the long term?
- Imagine a local law enforcement officer assigned to a JTTF listening to a wiretap under FISA. The officer hears a foreign-born terrorist discuss a series of past crimes. Because the wiretap was granted under FISA, the officer did not have probable cause to investigate criminal activity. A FISA court granted the wiretap for national security. What should the officer do? Would a criminal investigation jeopardize national security? Do you see any problems when the distinction between Title III and FISA wiretaps is blurred?
- Assume an Internet provider is arrested for refusing to turn over the records of a known foreign terrorist. The court dismisses the charges, saying this section of the Patriot Act is unconstitutional. What do you think might happened to other officers who arrested people for the same violation prior to this court decision?

---

gleaned from these warrants is not used in criminal prosecutions, but this is not the issue bothering Professor Herman. She compares FISA warrants to the type of surveillance proposed under the Patriot Act and concludes that the Patriot Act allows the government to watch its own citizens with similar rules. There is no guarantee such surveillance will exclude evidence used in criminal prosecutions.

The other part of Professor Herman's argument focuses on the relationship between executive and legislative powers, and she feels the Patriot Act concentrates too much power in the executive branch. The act gives the attorney general power to detain and deport aliens with less judicial review than was required prior to September 11, and the attorney general is only required to have reason to believe the action is necessary. Courts, she states, would require a much higher standard of proof. The Patriot Act also gives the attorney general and the secretary of state the power to designate certain associations as terrorist groups, and they may take actions against people and organizations associated with these groups. Herman believes Congress has failed to aggressively seek a role in the Patriot Act. By increasing executive powers, the Constitution is threatened. Her primary fear, she concludes, is that increased executive powers will be used to mask an attack on civil liberties.

BOX 2.5   Close-Up: Individual Rights and Life-Threatening Terrorism

Guaranteeing individual freedom is a difficult process. We tend to believe in freedom when:

- We agree with a concept;
- We're apathetic about the issue in question;
- We know the proponents of a particular position are powerless.

When our opponents touch our nerves and they have the ability to implement their views, it is difficult to maintain our view of basic rights. Examine the following summary of two segments of the al Qaeda manual. Do you feel these directives can be combated by aggressively insisting on the individual rights of captured suspected terrorists? Would al Qaeda give its victims basic individual rights? Does our system of individual rights separate us from violent, intolerant organizations?

SOURCE: al Qaeda manual

When captured:

- At trial insist you were tortured.
- Complain about mistreatment in prison.
- Learn the names of security officers and use them in court.
- Be willing to engage in a hunger strike.
- Pass information from prison.
- Hide messages to deliver to your brothers.
- When transported, shout Islamic phrases.

Gathering intelligence:

- Use open source information.
- Make friends and spy on them.
- It is permissible to beat hostages to obtain information.
- It is permissible to kill hostages if it works to your advantage.

The American Civil Liberties Union (ACLU, 3-20-02) voices other concerns with civil liberties. Citing increased executive powers to detain immigrants, the ACLU charges the attorney general with trying to "gut" immigration courts. The ACLU expresses two concerns. First, after September 11 the attorney general ordered the detention of several hundred immigrants. He refused to openly charge most of the detainees and refused to make the list known for several months. In addition, Attorney General Ashcroft sought to have the rules for detaining and deporting immigrants streamlined. He wanted to make the process more efficient by decreasing the amount of judicial review involved in immigration and naturalization cases. These issues incensed the ACLU.

Tightening immigration laws, the ACLU argues, is a smoke screen for increasing executive powers at the expense of individual rights. The ACLU believes the attorney general will rely on political issues rather than the rules of evidence when deciding which cases to prosecute. By streamlining immigration courts, there will be no judicial body to oversee executive decisions. The ACLU also believes President Bush will appoint judges sympathetic to Attorney General Ashcroft's views. This process undermines civil liberties, the ACLU says, at the expense of the Constitution.

To demonstrate the point, the ACLU points to the post–September 11 case of Ali Maqtari. Married to a member of the armed forces, Maqtari was driving his wife to Fort Campbell, Kentucky, when he was detained for questioning by federal agents and detained without probable cause to believe he had committed a crime. He was held for eight weeks without formal charges, according to the ACLU. After being granted a hearing, a court ruled that the government's position was unjustified. Maqtari was released. Without effective judicial review, the ACLU says, he may not have been released. Coming to grips with terrorism should not involve scrapping personal freedom contained in the Constitution.

Any attempt to utilize state and local law enforcement in intelligence-gathering operations will have constitutional implications. The police may be used in homeland security, but there are passionate and logical positions against this and equally powerful arguments supporting it. Regardless, even when the executive branch proposes a course of action, police operations will be influenced by court decisions. Local law enforcement's role in homeland defense cannot be developed in a constitutional vacuum.

3

Bureaucracy Problems

Law enforcement in the United States has been a haphazard affair on both national and local levels. Thomas Reppetto (1978) describes five styles of policing in America, each based on geographical and historical factors. On the federal level, regulatory and law enforcement agencies began to emerge in the Progressive Era (1890–1910), and the number of federal departments with law enforcement powers multiplied in the twentieth century. Intelligence agencies also have a scattered history. The Central Intelligence Agency (CIA) was formed after World War II (1939–1945) for the purpose of consolidating all defense intelligence, but the Director of Central Intelligence (DCI) never gained the authority to administer all military intelligence operations. After September 11, the Bush administration proposed new bureaucracies and offered plans for reorganizing old ones. Regardless of the outcome of these proposals, the relationship between homeland defense and policing will develop within the context of public bureaucracy.

After reading this chapter, you should be able to

1. Describe bureaucracy and its relationship to police work.
2. Draw an analogy between the issues in the Progressive Era and today's proposals for homeland defense.
3. Explain the need to reconceptualize policing, if law enforcement officers are to be used to gather intelligence.
4. Explain the logic of reconceptualizing the police role.
5. List and define the factors inhibiting changes in the police role.

BUREAUCRACIES: TWO VIEWS

If you have studied public administration or police management, you have most likely encountered the classic works on bureaucracy. Max Weber (1864–1920), one of the founding masters of sociology, coined the term "bureaucracy" to describe professional, rational organizations. For Weber, every aspect of organizational structure should be aimed at rationally producing goals. Labor is to be divided into specific functions or bureaus, and all functions or parts of the organization are to assemble logically to produce the whole. Management in the organization is rationally oriented, devoid of friendship, family, or political influences. Modern bureaucratic management ideally comes from leaders who excel at leadership. There is no place for inherited leadership or popular, elected managers in Weber's bureaucracy. Every aspect of the organization centers on rational efficiency (Weber, 1947). (See Box 3.1.)

Over a century has passed since Weber first outlined what would become known as bureaucratic organizational theory. To be sure, hundreds of other scholars have filled volumes with organizational theories and managerial texts. These works range from highly theoretical psychological treatises to practical business administration guides. The sheer number of these tracts indicates the issue at hand. Running an organization is a complicated affair, and the larger and more complex the organization becomes, the more difficult it is to manage (see Downs, 1967 and Warwick, 1975).

Law enforcement bureaucracies present no exception to modern organizational theories. Whether federal, state, or local, all police work is a political process occurring in the context of bureaucracy. Externally, police work takes

---

BOX 3.1 Close-Up: Critics of Public Bureaucracy

Critics level harsh attacks against public bureaucracies, and researchers have found differences between the ideal and practice of bureaucracy. Do you feel the following statements are correct?

- Bureaucracies work toward stagnation. Innovation, creativity, and individuality are discouraged.
- Career bureaucrats are rewarded with organizational power.
- Public bureaucracies do not face competition.
- It is better to make a safe decision than the correct decision.
- Bureaucratic organizations protect themselves when threatened with outside problems.

- Bureaucrats postpone decisions under the guise of gathering information.
- Policies and procedures are more important than outcomes in bureaucracies.
- Centralized bureaucracy increases paperwork.
- As bureaucracies grow, simple problems result in complex solutions.

Whether you agree with these criticisms or not, consider the problem from another vantage point. Is there an alternative to classic bureaucracy when organizing state and local police for homeland defense?

place within the American political system. It is a reflection of governmental power, and the actions of individual officers have political ramifications. Internally, conflicts arising from personal rivalries, territorial fights, and power struggles are as much a part of policing as they are in any organization (Gaines and Cordner, 1999, pp. 179–180; see also Walker, 1992). Both external and internal political realities will not disappear if the American police expand their role in homeland defense.

There are two views concerning expanded police bureaucracy. Supporters of one position maintain that consolidating police power is efficient. They argue that a large bureaucracy with a clear mission will empower the police to perform their mission. The latest manifestation of this position appears in the proposition to create a new cabinet-level homeland security office (Office of Homeland Security, 2002).

Proponents of a second position suggest that decentralizing police power personalizes services and develops links to communities. They believe localized offices are more adept at recognizing and handling problems. Support for this position can be found among those who seek to trim the homeland defense concept and those who favor limiting the involvement of state and local law enforcement in a larger organization. Although both ideas appear to be new in the wake of September 11, they are actually part of an ongoing issue as old as American law enforcement.

A NEW VERSION OF AN OLD ARGUMENT

Debates about the role of law enforcement in American government are as old as the police institution, and current thoughts on the police role in homeland defense represent a new variation on an old theme. To illustrate this point, it is possible to turn to the late nineteenth century when reformers became frustrated with attempts to centralize the authority of local law enforcement and turned to the idea of creating state police forces. The situation in Pennsylvania, in particular, illustrates this point.

America historians refer to the period between 1890 and 1910 as the "Progressive Era." Richard Hofstadter (1965), the dean of Progressive Era historians, cites the period as a time of reform and efficiency. Following Hofstadter's lead, mainstream historians see several common themes. Progressives attacked public corruption, government inefficiency, and social ills. Police historians like Samuel Walker (1977) and Thomas Reppetto (1978) see similar trends inside city police agencies. The Progressives formed alliances with moral reformers, business people, and government reformers to end corruption in police departments. Their cry was reform and their gospel was efficiency.

Revisionist historians such as Gabriel Kolko (1963) and James Weinstein (1968) take a different view. They argue that the Progressives created government regulations to rationalize the capitalist business climate. In other words, corrupt government was bad for business. Revisionist historians like Weinstein show a pattern of industrial leaders leaving business for regulatory positions and returning to industry in a cycle to support business, not good government.

Business leaders supported regulation when it created stable markets and discounted it when it only served the public good.

The real meaning of the Progressive Era probably lies between the position of mainstream historians and that of the revisionists, but the ideas of good government and moral reform intersected with business interests in the coal fields of Pennsylvania around 1905. Elbert Gary, the president of U.S. Steel, had a problem. Strikes among coal miners interrupted the flow of coal to Pittsburgh steel mills, completely disrupting production and profits. The coal industry had a particularly violent labor history involving murder, revolutionary activity, and violent repression. By 1905 Gary reconciled himself to the presence of labor unions, but he wanted to put an end to illegal strikes that deprived his steel mills of coal (McConnell, 1970, p. 56).

Gary and other industrial leaders had three tools to deal with illegal labor actions. They could lobby the government to deploy the National Guard to police industry or ask local governments to utilize city and county law enforcement agencies to arrest violent labor leaders and protect replacement workers. Both of these actions, however, were indirect and ineffective. Since local police officers and guardsmen came from the working class, they frequently identified with striking workers. Industrialists were left with the option of deploying private police who, even though they were used frequently, failed to stabilize production due to their murderous tactics. The industrialists needed another option.

Realizing the predicament, Gary approached his friend President Theodore Roosevelt. Playing to Roosevelt's infatuation with the Rough Riders, Gary convinced the president to support the creation of permanent Pennsylvania State Troops with full police powers. The Pennsylvania State Police was born in 1905 (Conti, 1977, pp. 1–29).

Industrialists and reformers applauded the state police movement and pointed to Pennsylvania as a model for the rest of the nation. Organized along strict military lines, the police were efficient and effective. Avoiding overt corruption, they responded to crimes throughout the entire state. More importantly for the industrialists, the state police could respond to strikes. When miners or other laborers set up a picket line, they were confronted by trained police personnel.

The anti-labor role prompted another view of the state police. The Pennsylvania Federation of Labor responded to the new troops with horror. The state police were, the labor activists said, American Cossacks. Trained and militarized, their purpose was to terrorize and regulate workers. While they could not rely on local police and the National Guard, industrial leaders could count on the state police to keep workers in line (Pennsylvania Federation of Labor, 1915).

Samuel Walker (1975) dichotomizes American police historiography into a heroic school praising police bravery and a critical school exposing both positive and negative aspects in law enforcement history. While both of these positions can be seen in the historiography of the state police movement, there is a more subtle lesson dealing with homeland security. The state police movement was successful because President Roosevelt, a former New York City Police Commissioner frustrated with the failure of good government progressives to centralize police authority, threw his full weight behind the concept (see Gibson, 1974). In one way, Roosevelt's actions superceded local activity by creating a new bureaucracy, although it must be remembered that he also had a powerful alliance forged by Gary supporting the movement.

There are parallels with the federal call for homeland security and debates about state policing a century ago. The homeland security proposal (Office of Homeland Security, 2002, p. ix) calls for cooperation with state and local police. While the Constitution says powers not granted to the federal government are reserved for the states, the security proposal says *all levels of government—federal, state, and local—will work together* (Ibid., p. 33, italics mine). In defense of the administration's proposal, many state and local agencies are anxious to cooperate with the proposed federal security system, and the proposal wants to "enable effective partnerships with state and local governments and the private sector." The plan does not mandate federally administered relationships. By the same token, the essential questions raised by the proposal have striking paral-

---

BOX 3.2 Close-Up: Law Enforcement Highlights from Homeland Security

The Office of Homeland Security forwarded the following ideas and suggestions:

- Terrorism requires cooperation among all levels of government.
- The federal government should offer suggestions, not mandates for state and local governments.
- Federalism involves state governments sharing power with the federal government.
- The federal government recognizes 87,000 differing governmental jurisdictions within the United States.
- The purpose of Homeland Security is to develop cooperative governmental systems rather than duplication.
- Police reform should improve law enforcement coordination among all levels of government.
- The FBI needs to be restructured to meet security needs.
- Infrastructure protection should be coordinated with law enforcement.
- Law enforcement and intelligence agencies should share intelligence.

- Police agencies and businesses should protect against inside threats.
- Local and federal emergency response plans should be coordinated.
- The federal government will create a national incident management system.
- Federal and local governments will build a citizen corps.
- Military forces will plan to support civil authority.
- States should adopt minimum standards for driver's licenses.
- All levels of government will coordinate to suppress money laundering.
- The federal government will support the continuity of courts.
- The federal government will create "smart borders."
- The federal government will revitalize the United States Coast Guard.

President Bush signed the Homeland Security Bill on November 25, 2002, revamping federal law enforcement and its role with state and local agencies.

SOURCE: National Strategy for Homeland Security, July 2002.

lels with the Progressive Era. Will police functions be centralized? Is efficiency the measure of police effectiveness? Will homeland defense result in a new type of police force or level of policing? Will state and local law enforcement remain autonomous?

The purpose of this section is not to answer these questions but to point to the continuing issue of competing philosophies about bureaucracy in police history. While the state police movement provided centralized, efficient law enforcement or traffic agencies in most states, it also resulted in the problem of overlapping jurisdiction. State agencies might be efficient in their own organization, but complexity in the overall law enforcement structure grew, and the creation of dozens of federal law enforcement and regulatory agencies added to the confusion. In a nutshell, overlapping, autonomous law enforcement and regulatory bureaucracies share the same jurisdictions, partially as a result of the Progressive movement. It is not unusual to have the same jurisdiction served by a state police agency, a county sheriff, and a local police department. Each agency has its own leadership, its own structure, and its own system of accountability. (See Box 3.2.)

The Bush administration is not seeking to replicate history. In the homeland security proposal sent to Congress, the government is calling for full participation by state and local agencies. If homeland security results in a new police bureaucracy, it will compete with existing bureaucracies. If it seeks to develop cooperative relationships with existing police agencies, homeland defense managers need to negotiate power sharing arrangements with state and local police.

RETHINKING POLICE WORK

It is possible to use state and local police agencies in homeland defense. On the most rudimentary level, officers could be assigned to security tasks and trained to look for information beyond the violation of criminal law. On a more sophisticated level, police intelligence units could be established to gather and pass on intelligence information. As discussed in Chapter 1, utilizing the police in defense operations would mean redefining the *de facto* role of law enforcement, but it could be done. The most effective initial practice would be to train patrol officers, investigators, and narcotics officers to look for indicators of terrorism during their daily activities. The central question is, Do Americans want to redirect police crime-fighting efforts toward intelligence gathering? (See Box 3.3.)

The process of gathering defense intelligence is not readily apparent in American policing. Most law enforcement officers did not enter police ranks thinking that they were joining an army. Their motivation generally focuses on the elimination of crime, not national defense. In addition, local police policies and employment incentives reinforce their original notions. Officers are encouraged to maintain a local view, and police managers reinforce pragmatic actions while discouraging abstract thinking. Police work is extremely political, and law enforcement officers think locally. To paraphrase former Speaker of the House Tip O'Neill's maxim, "All law enforcement politics are local." The goal is not to alienate constituencies, but to develop deep community ties

---

BOX 3.3   Close-Up: Asking New Questions—Seeking New Answers

If state and local law enforcement officers were to begin looking for signs of terrorism, they would need to frame basic questions about adversaries. For example, in addition to criminal briefings before patrol or investigative tours, officers would need to think of questions such as:

- What is the M.O. of our enemy?
- How does the enemy's organization function?

- What types of tactics will the enemy use?
- What types of weapons will the enemy use?
- How can information be gathered while protecting the source?
- What community indicators give the answers to questions 1–4?
- How can information be shared securely with other agencies?

---

to keep information flowing. Information translates to organizational power and it solves crimes (Manning, 1977, p. 35).

State and local officers are not rewarded for thinking in terms of international issues or national security. Chiefs and sheriffs do not usually praise abstract reasoning. In an early critique of collegiate criminal justice programs, Lawrence Sherman (1978) claims that higher education has done little to help this situation. Criminal justice programs do not produce abstract, critical thinkers for law enforcement, Sherman believes; they impart skills. According to a recent survey by *Police: The Law Enforcement Magazine*, graduates steeped in academic preparation are not as welcome in law enforcement agencies as recruits with military experience (July 2002). Discipline and the willingness to obey orders are more important than individual thinking and creativity.

Modern terrorism is an abstract nebulous concept fluctuating according to historical and political circumstances. To combat terrorism, security forces require groups of people with abstract reasoning skills, knowledge of international politics and history, and specialized expertise in particular regions (Betts, 2002). If the police are to participate as full partners in this process, they must bring skilled specialists to the table. The ethos behind policing, however, rejects this logic. American law enforcement relishes pragmatic information with immediate applicability on the beat.

Localized attitudes bring contempt from intelligence agencies. Unlike analysts in defense intelligence, state and local police officers frequently exhibit no concern for in-depth background information, the kind of information needed to understand intelligence. As a result, intelligence bureaucracies frequently question police competence. Intelligence analysts know information is not usually valuable until it is categorized and placed within social and political contexts. If police agencies are unable to engage in this type of examination, intelligence organizations are hesitant to form partnerships with them.

Before being too critical of local law enforcement, it is helpful to recall the function of police intelligence. While it has evolved in a patchwork of patterns, state and local law enforcement agencies have been generally excluded from noncriminal intelligence gathering, and since the COINTELPRO scandal, many of them have been legally banned from doing so. If state and local police agencies are to move into homeland defense, new rules and norms for intelligence gathering need to be developed. It is important to remember that any such issues will be subject to judicial review and interpretation.

THE LOGIC OF RECONCEPTUALIZING THE POLICE ROLE

The organizational processes inhibiting law enforcement intelligence gathering and sharing do not eliminate police participation in homeland defense. On the contrary, they can be identified and solved. Many alternatives can be developed. For example, rather than bringing police officers into the intelligence process as full partners, it is possible to train them to recognize the practical signs of terrorism. In other words, police officers could be trained to look for indicators of terrorism and to pass the information along.

Another alternative for state and local agencies is to combine training in alertness with specialized training for selected officers. Rather than bringing an entire department into intelligence-gathering operations, select units could engage in counterterrorist activities. This is the logic behind the FBI's Joint Terrorism Task Force (JTTF). As described in Chapter 1, these units combine local, state, and various federal police officers, as well as corrections officials and prosecutors, in regional units designed to combat terrorism. Local and state officers are given federal authority, while the presence of state and local officers gives federal agents the ability to act in local jurisdictions. The JTTFs have been effective in many cases (Watson, 2002).

In addition to specialized units, state and local law enforcement can assume the role of becoming eyes and ears for intelligence forces. This may be the least costly endeavor, although, as you previously read, it raises concerns from both civil libertarians and others who strongly espouse local control of the American police. If it were to be invoked, officers on various levels would need to be trained to be alert for anti-terrorist information while performing their routine duties.

Counterterrorism begins with basic information. It is not some exotic notion straight out of the latest James Bond movie. Law enforcement gets too confused by bureaucratic rules and regulations, a misunderstanding of intelligence, and its own fetish for secrecy. Good information comes from everyday sources, and intelligence gathering is often nothing more than good police work. The keys are knowing what to look for and knowing when, where, and how to share information. (See Box 3.4.)

One need only look at the record to demonstrate this point. In domestic terrorism, the first person on the scene is usually a local police officer. Any seasoned investigator knows that the actions of the first officer on the scene are critical to the case. The process does not stop at the crime scene. A major break in the case against the Symbionese Liberation Army came when a Michigan State trooper happened to make a traffic stop. It was an example of aggressive patrol. The trooper was stopping violators as a method of aggressive crime prevention. It would be well to remember that Oklahoma City bomber Timothy McVeigh was

---

BOX 3.4   Close-Up: Patrol Observations

If state and local law enforcement become involved in intelligence gathering, patrol officers should look for the following:

- Sudden expansion of violent groups and rhetoric
- Suspects who have money with no furnishings in apartments

- Disputes among close knit groups
- Radical literature
- Hand-drawn maps
- Loitering around sensitive areas
- Loud and boisterous behavior in tight-knit groups
- Alienated groups in school settings

BOX 3.5   Close Up: Investigative Observations

If state and local officers become involved in intelligence gathering, investigators and narcotics officers should look for the following:

- Links to bootlegging schemes where profits are funneled to an organization or foreign country
  —Cigarette tax fraud schemes
  —Baby formula distribution schemes
  —Grocery store coupons fraud

- Protection rackets with money channeled to a group or foreign country
- Search warrants
  —Make sure warrants include seizure of written records, computers, cell phones
- Connections outside jurisdictions
- Donations to charities
- Narcotics trafficking to raise funds for an organization
- Clean drug labs that may be bomb factories

---

also stopped by a state patrol officer who noticed something amiss. These examples are not glorified cases. They are the results of aggressive patrol. (See Box 3.5.)

The American police are in a perfect position to engage in intelligence gathering activities and expand their role in national defense. Other Western democracies have done this quite successfully, including France and Germany. The Canadians and British accomplished the same thing while keeping more of a public service model than the French or the Germans. The defensive role can be formalized, but many factors inhibit the process.

FACTORS INHIBITING CHANGES
IN THE POLICE ROLE

Unlike the ideal rational organizations envisioned by Weber, public service organizations have foibles that emerge in the everyday social construction of reality. Personalities are important, varying levels of competency limit or expand effectiveness, and organizations tend to act in their own interest. If all the organizations involved in homeland defense agree to pool their efforts, several bureaucratic hurdles need to be cleared (see Swanson, Territo, and Taylor, 2001, pp. 643–644; Best, 12-3-01; Bodrero, 2002; and Mitchell and Hulse, 6-27-02). Some of the important issues include the following.

FBI versus Police and Sheriffs Departments

In October 2001, FBI Director Robert Mueller attended the International Association of Chiefs of Police Meeting in Toronto, Ontario. According to chiefs who attended the meeting, it was not a pleasant experience. State and local law enforcement executives criticized Director Mueller for failing to share information. According to several private comments from FBI agents, Director Mueller returned vowing this would never happen again. American law enforcement would witness a new FBI. Despite the intentions of the most forceful bureaucratic leaders, orders do not always go as planned. There have been success stories with information sharing, but there have also been tales of woe. Many American police executives are not convinced the FBI is in partnership with efforts to stop terrorism (Levitt, 1-28-02).

The purpose here is not to condemn the FBI, but to acknowledge a bureaucratic issue. Many state and local police executives do not trust the FBI, and the attitude extends down through the ranks of law enforcement agencies. If the American police are to become part of homeland defense, the relationship between the FBI and state and local law enforcement must be improved (Riordan and Zegart, 7-5-02).

Federal Law Enforcement Rivalries

Unfortunately, federal law enforcement agencies mistrust one another at times. While not directly related to state and local issues, their failure to cooperate in some circumstances influences local police relationships. Many federal law enforcement agencies openly resent the FBI, and this attitude is frequently reciprocated. In addition, the creation of new bureaucracies such as the Transportation Security Administration (TSA) exacerbates rivalries. In the real world of bureaucracy, organizations on every level frequently act out of self-interest rather than concern with the overall mission (Valburn, 2-4-02).

Advocates of Local Control

Some people feel cooperation between state and local law enforcement will result in the *de facto* concentration of police power. This attitude was alive and well during the state police debates at the turn of the last century, and it continues to live in various forms. Civil libertarians believe that consolidated police power will serve to erode civil rights. Local government officials worry that their agendas will be lost in federalization. The bureaucratic arguments extend beyond these interest groups (Hitt and Cloud, 6-10-02).

The Problem of Legal Bureaucracy

Another factor inhibiting police cooperation is the legal bureaucracy of criminal justice. Samuel Walker (1985) points out that the criminal justice system is actually not a system at all, but a multifaceted bureaucracy with intersecting layers. He refers to the process quite humorously as the "wedding cake model." Rather than a smooth flow among police, courts, and corrections, Walker sees a model based on plea bargaining, celebrated cases, and long-term punishment for the worst offenders.

Each entity in the criminal justice system is independent, although it interacts with the other parts. There is no overall leader, and law enforcement, courts, and correctional agencies refuse to accept single management. From the Constitution's perspective, the courts are hardly designed to fit into a criminal justice system. While police and correctional institutions represent the executive branch of government, the courts autonomously belong to the judicial branch (del Carmen, 1991, pp. 275–277). Efforts to increase the efficiency of homeland defense will not change these relationships.

THE BUREAUCRACY PROBLEM

In June 2002, President George Bush proposed what he described as the largest overhaul of government since the Cold War. The purpose of his proposed reforms was to increase the efficiency and effectiveness of homeland defense. While his description of the proposal may have been correct, the federal government cannot assume the reforms will carry over into the state and local governments. The states may cooperate with the federal government, but they are not mandated to do so. The states and their local governments have established, entrenched bureaucracies with their own managerial structures and agendas. These organizations will not suddenly change methods of operation simply because centralized executive authority has mandated new policies for homeland defense. In a nutshell, this is the epitome of the "bureaucracy problem," yet it does not imply that state and local governments will automatically reject chances to participate. Change can happen, and may even be welcome, if federal agencies enter into cooperative relationships with their local counterparts (Liptak, 5-31-02; see also Downs, 1967 and Warwick, 1975).

Some advocates believe federal reform has pointed the way. A 1995 attempt to reduce paper work in federal government is one example. An earlier effort came in the 1978 Civil Service Reform Act where special executives were given managerial authority and placed in performance-based positions. Yet, managing homeland security will still require attention to the issues raised in this chapter. Large organizations are difficult to manage, and problems increase rapidly when organizational effectiveness requires cooperation on several levels. Homeland security calls for new alliances among federal agencies and cooperative relations among local, state, and federal levels of government. In addition, police officers need to think beyond their local jurisdictions and common crimes, if they are to participate in national defense. Power bureaucrats and bureaucratic procedures do not change easily. It can be done, but it becomes a massive political and managerial task.

4

On Police Work in the Clausewitzian Paradigm

Constitutional issues and bureaucratic problems will modify the structure of homeland defense, but the force behind the quest for domestic security is international terrorism. The terrorists of September 11 operated in a quasi–military manner, employing trained operatives to attack civilian targets without an open declaration of war. Although political rhetoric and sensationalistic news reports declare that America is at war, scholars like Michael Howard (2002) suggest that we are in an emergency situation not quite meeting the standard of war. The problem, as terrorist analysts have long known, is not war per se, but subnational conflict. It is something more than ordinary crime and something less than conventional war. If America were involved in standard crime, law enforcement power would suffice. If the issue were war between states, American military forces could respond. America, however, is involved in a low-level conflict, a war in the shadows with few well-defined battle zones. The shadow war demands a variety of responses, utilizing sometimes strange combinations of defense and law enforcement forces. This is problematic because the purpose of police agencies, especially on the local level, is not "to provide for the common defense," and local officers are seldom able to place information within an international political context. Yet a war in the shadows requires law enforcement to understand something about the nature of conflict. Before continuing the discussion of homeland defense, it is important to consider some of the aspects of war and the way it is manifested in the shadows.

After reading this chapter, you should be able to

1. Discuss war as a science and an art.
2. Summarize the nebulous nature of low-level conflict.

3. Outline some military principles from Clausewitz and Sun Tzu.

4. Describe the nature of asymmetrical warfare.

5. Encapsulate Hoffman's summary of asymmetrical revolts.

6. Summarize historical and legal issues complicating the use of police agencies in national defense.

7. Define Manning's analysis of the mandate and describe how this further confuses potential roles in national defense.

8. Outline events that may force state and local law enforcement to rethink Clausewitzian concepts of war.

SCIENCE AND ART

War is an ever changing event. Successful conflict requires innovation, ruthlessness, and surprise. Some strategists debate whether war is a science or an art, but in reality it combines both ideas. There are certain principles that scientifically dominate war—massing troops, supplying them, concentrating forces against an enemy, and surprising the opponent—and they may be mastered through study. By the same token, the application of principles is an artistic process. The same commanders with the same conditions can produce differing results. Inspired and intuitive commanders win battles, if they understand the art of war.

Martin van Creveld (1985, pp. 270–273) explains the interplay between art and science. Throughout the history of war, van Creveld says, the most successful commanders have been those who did not turn their troops into automatons. They selected troops for particular missions and gave them the freedom to make autonomous decisions through the course of a campaign or battle. The result of war is not technological determinism, but freedom to act with innovation as the situation demands. Despite growing communication systems and the desire to exercise control, successful commanders master the principles of war and apply them with artistic freedom.

The art of war is not static, and the years following World War II (1939–1945) brought new meanings to fields of conflict—meanings demanding new and innovative responses. Modern terrorism emerged from this period, beginning with anticolonial revolts and guerrilla wars in the years immediately following the Second World War. Urban terrorism followed the anticolonial phase and it grew into an international affair. These new terrorists encompassed left-wing groups in the West and Latin America and nationalistic terrorists in the West and Asia. Middle Eastern terrorism reemerged in the 1970s in the wake of the leftist and nationalist period. By the 1990s, terrorism was increasingly a religious affair. No matter what form terrorism took, however, successful terrorists did not seek decisive World War II-style confrontations. They never assumed they were operating in peace time but believed they were perpetually at war. Western democracies, by contrast, made legal distinctions between peace and war.

Even when war is undeclared, both governments and terrorists use war as a metaphor for their actions. Terrorists like the metaphor because it glorifies their causes and leaders. In addition, terrorists find military planning convenient. Governments use references to war because it grants them greater leeway when acting outside the law. Western governments in particular see war as a legal issue producing a code of behavior distinct from peace. This presents a philosophical problem.

THE NEBULOUS NATURE

OF LOW-INTENSITY CONFLICT:

CLAUSEWITZ AND SUN TZU

Prior to the time of growing terrorism, Americans seemed to know the meaning of conflict. War was an extension of politics fought within the legal framework of the Constitution. Quite simply, the Constitution states that only Congress has the power to declare war, and Congress declares whether America is in a state of war or peace. However, the anticolonial struggles following World War II, the Vietnam War, and battles in Somalia and Serbia confused the issue for the military: American troops were killed in peacetime. To confuse the situation even further, civil agencies responded to a bombing in Oklahoma City, two teenagers on a shooting spree at Columbine High School, and suicide attacks on September 11. Clearly, the police were not soldiers, but they were being called to military-style attacks.

Although criticized in the wake of Germany's defeat in 1945, Western military planning has been influenced by Carl von Clausewitz's military philosophy (1984; orig. 1831; for critiques see Liddell Hart, 1967; Craig, 1968; and Howard, 1988). Clausewitz cut his teeth during the nationalistic wars against Napoleon (1795–1815). Joining the Prussian Army as a twelve-year-old drummer boy, he fought under the Duke of Brunswick against the French Revolution. Clausewitz noted the Prussians won almost every engagement with the French revolutionary army, but the French always seemed to regroup and stand ready to fight. The French, young Clausewitz thought, were fighting for their nation, while the Prussians were fighting for a king. The French Revolution had produced a new type of war.

Clausewitz began to study war as a philosophical problem. The strength of the French came from their ability to place the nation in arms. To defeat the French, Germany must unite under a democracy and employ its own citizen soldiers. The proof of victory would come when his nation's will could be imposed on its enemies. Clausewitz joined a group of reformers and attempted to modernize the Prussian Army. The Prussians were destroyed, however, in 1806 after the Battle of Jena-Auerstadt, and Clausewitz was carried off to Paris in captivity with a Prussian prince. He began writing—formulating a philosophy of national war.

BOX 4.1   Close-Up: *On War*, Carl von Clausewitz

Clausewitz's ideas did not gain popularity among German military commanders until shortly before the First World War (1914–1918). By the same token, his treatise of the nation-in-arms was accepted by many military theorists. Examine some of these paraphrased conclusions of Clausewitz.

- A nation is either at war or at peace.
- The purpose of diplomacy is to impose your will on your enemy.
- When diplomacy has failed, war may result.
- War must unite the will and resources of the nation.

- War is to be waged with maximum violence to destroy the enemy's will to fight.
- Battle results from a mutual decision to fight.
- All resources should be aimed at the main point (*Schwerpunkt*) of the battle to decisively defeat the enemy.
- War plans should be aimed at the total defeat of the enemy.

Are these conclusions applicable to terrorism? Should domestic terrorism be countered as if it were a war? Is a struggle against foreign-inspired terrorism a war in Clausewitz's sense? Do most American's think about war as Clausewitz did?

Clausewitz's notions were derived from his study of history, especially the Thirty Years' War (1618–1648) and Frederick the Great (1740–1786). They were also influenced by his decision to join the Russian Army in 1812 to fight Napoleon and the German War of Liberation (1813–1814). Clausewitz's ideas come to us from a book published by his wife Maria the year after he died. *On War* is a philosophical treatise on the nature of total, nationalistic wars. It has also been one of the most influential works on military forces in the twentieth century. The problem for American law enforcement is not Clausewitz's understanding of the nation-in-arms, but the changing structure of conflict. (See Box 4.1.)

Victor Hanson (1989) criticizes Clausewitz and the Western way of battle for focusing on warfare in ancient Greece. According to this line of thought, the purpose of military action is to seek a decisive engagement, and Clausewitz's philosophical treatise emphasizes this point. Terrorism is designed to produce the opposite effect, seeking to avoid a direct confrontation with force. In addition, since the emergence of professional, modern warfare in the West after the Peace of Westphalia (1648), the purpose of war has been to impose political will on the defeated party. American law enforcement does not seek a decisive battle with enemy forces, and its purpose can never be the imposition of political will. The goals of terrorism are to create panic and cause social systems to break. While the police have been called to the Clausewitzian paradigm, where America is either at war or at peace, another frame of reference may be more helpful.

Nearly 2000 years ago a Chinese philosopher, Sun Tzu, produced a treatise on the paradoxes of war (Management Analytics, 1995). Rather than conceiving of times when a political realm is at war or at peace, Sun Tzu saw war and peace as two sides of the same coin. War and politics were psychological forces held together by the belief in power. In Sun Tzu's philosophical structure, the highest form of military leadership comes in breaking the enemy's resistance without fighting. Leaders must be able to control their anger and project power. When military leadership is strong, the state will be strong and have less need to act. If the state appears to be weak, it is vulnerable despite its strength.

Clausewitz wrote at a time of emerging nationalism, constitutions, and democracies. It was a time when military victory involved creating mass armies for the delivery of a decisive blow, and even though Communist interpreters of Clausewitz saw peace as another means of war, Clausewitz saw war and peace as legal matters. A nation was either at peace or at war. Writing in another era in another civilization, Sun Tzu saw few dichotomies between war and peace. A state projected power both in war and in peace, and its power could be threatened by public perceptions. In a time of low-level conflict, it may be wise for law enforcement agencies to consider some ancient Chinese concepts of power and warfare. (See Box 4.2.)

Nebulous conflicts have become a problem for Western democracies (Howard, 2002). In the face of growing terrorism, domestic unrest, and subnational warfare, one of the greatest challenges to the structure of Western democracies may well be the need to augment military force with civilian police power. Referring to this as a "Security Force" concept, Crozier (1975) argues that combined military and police operations are becoming commonplace. The ironic aspect of this position is that rule through combined police-military power is the norm for totalitarian states. Wilkinson (1974, Chapters 1 and 2) refers to this condition as state terrorism. The paradox is apparent. The extent

---

BOX 4.2   Close-Up: Paraphrasing Sun Tzu

Compare the selected paraphrases of Sun Tzu with those of Clausewitz. Which statements are more applicable to conventional battles with frontlines and uniformed soldiers? Which statements are more applicable to guerrilla war and terrorism?

- If you know yourself and your enemy, you will be successful. If you know yourself and do not know your enemy, you will fail many times. If you know neither yourself nor your enemy, you will never succeed.

- The worst way to take a town is to lay siege. The best way is to make the inhabitants believe they are beaten.
- A military leader who projects strength can settle a dispute without losing a soldier.
- The best leader subdues the enemy's troops without fighting.
- Reduce the enemy by creating problems, making trouble, and making them rush to any given point.

SOURCE: *http://www.all.net/books/tzu.html.*

to which civilian legal authority can be used to counter political threats while maintaining free institutions and individual rights may have been in the minds of the framers of the United States Constitution, and the concept is certainly a dominant topic today.

ASYMMETRICAL WARFARE

Terrorism is based on Sun Tzu's concept of strength-to-weakness, not the strength-to-strength battle as Clausewitz described. In modern military parlance this is called asymmetry. Asymmetry simply means competing forces are out of balance; that is, a weak force fights a much stronger power. A good analogy is to think of a single angry hornet attacking a hiker in the woods. The angry hornet can sting the hiker, and if it is extremely lucky, cause the hiker to panic or maybe induce a fatal allergic reaction. If the hiker stays calm, however, a single swat ends the attack. The odds are in the hiker's favor. Terrorists are much like the imaginary hornet with two exceptions. They tend to be true-believing fanatics who sacrifice the lives of others to carry on a struggle with a superior force, and they have a better chance of striking when avoiding social conventions and societal norms. In other words, terrorists fight outside the rules.

Terrorism is a tactic of weakness. When a disadvantaged population strikes a more privileged class, it lacks the ability to confront the other group on an equal level. Just as it lacks economic and political power in the face of the dominant group, it also lacks military power. This is a problem for most revolutionary forces and weak powers attempting to fight a stronger force. A weak power cannot attack a stronger nation directly. It must use unconventional methods of fighting and attack the stronger force indirectly, many times striking nontraditional civilian targets.

The reason terrorists fight outside the norms of society is revealed by the imbalance of power. The major powers hold all the cards in international trade, legal authority, and military power. It does no good to strike them in the open, but they are vulnerable when attacked outside the norms of standard international relations. The lesson is as old as terrorism. The rule is, "If you can't kill their soldiers, kill their civilians." The purpose of asymmetry is to give the impression that powerful economic, military, and political forces cannot protect ordinary people going about daily routines. Terrorists do not seek an open battle but want to show that the norms of civil society cannot protect the population of the superior force. Enemy forces prepared for combat are too strong, but police stations, off-duty military personnel, and schoolchildren make tempting targets.

Asymmetry works only when terrorist infrastructures remain hidden, and concealment gives terrorists strength. If their bases are open or if they overestimate their strength, a superior power is able to reverse the asymmetrical process and engage terrorists on its own terms. This is the reason terrorists fight in the shadows. If state and local police agencies join the asymmetrical fight, their primary strength is the ability to collect information. Information allows security forces to bring terrorists into the open, and it is the key to counterterrorism. Intelligence gathering assumes the most important function in asymmetrical war.

Hoffman's Analysis of Asymmetry

Few scholars have summarized asymmetrical war better than St. Andrew's professor Bruce Hoffman, one of the foremost terrorism experts of our day. Hoffman (1998, pp. 45–65) points to the changing nature of war in the past fifty years. He notes that the fall of European colonial possessions to the Japanese in the Second World War established a revolutionary idea throughout the colonial world. Japanese conquest proved Europeans and their systems were not inherently superior to native populations in Africa, Asia, and Latin America. Prior to defeating Germany, European powers signed a declaration asserting the right of nations to control their political destinies, and European colonies took up the cry in the form of political revolt after 1945.

As violence spread across European colonies, revolutionary leaders quickly realized they could not fight Europeans in a conventional manner. European armies were simply too strong. As a result, revolutionaries found their strategy guided by other principles. The purpose, they reasoned, was not to win a military confrontation against a superior power; their goal was to win a political battle in the court of public opinion. The art of war required a shift in the application of age-old principles, and modern terrorism was born.

Hoffman (1998, pp. 45–65) examines three anticolonial revolts, in Palestine, Cyprus, and Algeria, to demonstrate the effectiveness of asymmetry. In Palestine two Jewish terrorist groups, the Irgun Zvai Leumi and the Stern Gang, found they could attack the occupying British forces even though the British outnumbered them. The keys to terrorist successes were threefold: (1) terrorists looked and acted as normal citizens when not engaged in combat, (2) terrorists operated in an urban environment allowing them to emerge from a crowd and to merge back into it, and (3) symbolic targets created an aura around each attack, making it appear to be more significant than it really was. Terrorists demonstrated that superior numbers of British soldiers could not keep the country safe.

Long before the twenty-four-hour news coverage of CNN, Hoffman argues, Zionist terrorists were able to focus world attention on a relatively obscure cause. When the terrorists murdered Palestinian Arabs or British soldiers, they did so for the sake of gaining notoriety. They hoped to wear the security forces down psychologically, to create a political climate in Britain that would deem the costs of occupying Palestine to be too high, and to keep the conflict before the eyes of the world. When the British left in 1948 it was partially as a result of a successful terrorist campaign. Other revolutionaries took note: asymmetrical war worked.

Hoffman's analysis of Cyprus and Algeria reveals similar results. Cypriot terrorists had no desire to kill British soldiers for the purpose of gaining a military victory. They wanted to demonstrate the ability of a weaker force to strike a stronger force. It was asymmetrical war. The same lesson came into play in Algeria. One Algerian revolutionary stated that it was better to kill one enemy in front of the world's media than it was to kill ten in a forsaken desert. The purpose of killing was to gain attention. In addition, terrorism in Palestine, Cyprus, and Algeria legitimized civilian targets. Murdering civilians had the same impact as killing soldiers.

Many analysts believe modern terrorism evolved from these colonial revolts. Anticolonialism gave way to left-wing and ethnic violence in the 1960s and 1970s. As left-wing and nationalistic violence swept the Middle East, Asia, Latin America, and the West, an international ethos of revolutionary terrorism seemed to pit itself against the Western world. Carlos Marighella espoused theories of terrorist revolution in *The Minimanual of the Urban Guerrilla* and *For the Liberation of Brazil,* and some analysts spoke of a terrorist international while others looked for state sponsors. The former Soviet Union's defeat in Afghanistan (1979–1989) introduced a new facet into the logic of asymmetrical war: religion. In essence, the world was experiencing the continually changing nature of war. For the most part, technologically and numerically superior armies were called to fight an illusive enemy in the shadows.

BOX 4.3   Close-Up: Asymmetry in Afghanistan

In December 1979 the former Soviet Union invaded Afghanistan to support a puppet Communist regime, resulting in a devastating ten year war. Seven differing groups of Islamic holy warriors (mujahideen) launched a guerrilla war against the Soviets, and young radical Muslims from Morocco to Indonesia flocked to the cause. Osama bin Laden was one of them, and al Qaeda was born in the midst of the guerrilla war. The United States funneled money and arms to the mujahideen through Pakistan's Inter-Service Intelligence (ISI) agency. The ISI, in turn, not only supported the mujahideen but many violent radical groups with links to the United States, such as al Qaeda and Jamaat al Fuqra.

The Soviets left Afghanistan in December 1989, but no single mujahideen group brought order to the war-torn country. Afghanistan disintegrated into violent anarchy with local warlords vying for control of various portions of the land. Eventually, young puritanical Islamic students known as the Taliban came to power.

Bin Laden's mujahideen reassembled in various guises during the United States' first war with Iraq. Al Qaeda moved to Afghanistan in 1996 and issued a "declaration of war" against the West and the Jewish people. The terrorist organization could survive in Afghanistan because of the country's relative anarchy and because the Taliban was not strong enough to confront al Qaeda. Bin Laden established training bases and terrorist training schools while increasing al Qaeda's strength. United States' military forces destroyed al Qaeda's command structure in the fall of 2001, but autonomous sleeper cells remained in over sixty countries after the fighting wound down.

Asymmetry is not a new concept in war. In fact, the purpose of battle is to bring more resources, troops, and power to a point where the enemy lacks resources, troops, and power. Successful military leaders create asymmetrical situations. It makes little sense for terrorists to fight in the open against a superior force, and the same logic can be applied to troops who fight terrorists. There are times when conventional military tactics can be used to destroy terrorist bases, but there are other times when information gathering, criminal investigation, and arrest are far more effective. Michael Howard (2002) argues this point effectively when discussing counterterrorist operations. Counterterrorism, he says, takes place in quiet intelligence operations, secretive strikes, and the elimination of selected targets. Counterterrorism is asymmetrical by implication. In other words, when an enemy strikes your weakness, learn to fight with your strength and bring the right weapons to the right fight. (See Box 4.3.)

LOCAL POLICE HISTORY
AND THE DEFENSE FUNCTION

Traditionally, the American police and the criminal justice system have had no role in national defense, with the exception of a few federal level operations. While guerilla war, terrorism, and subnational conflicts are nothing new in history (in fact, there are many instances where limited warfare dominated international relations), Brian Jenkins (1983) argues that low-intensity conflict assumes a major role in modern war. The police are, in terms of functional definition, a domestic force exercising powers of civil arrest and social control. Indeed, conventional wisdom suggests that even if the art of war has presented new dimensions to planners, civil police powers are divorced from the process.

The American criminal justice system has a distinct heritage in Western civilization emerging from two traditions. First, there is a legal heritage, which grew from a body of Roman, Anglo-Saxon common, and case laws. The guiding light for the application of these laws is the Constitution of the United States. A second tradition involving enforcement of the law grew from military roots, and it did not evolve from a legal heritage. While the legal system is concerned about the individual's relationship to the state, the enforcement system is concerned with state power. It is important to recognize both the military origins of police power and its separation from the legal system. Many people erroneously assume that the courts and police emerged from the same roots. As agents of state it is the police system, not the legal system, that operationalizes state power (Blumberg, 1979, pp. 86–97).

Despite its military origins, law enforcement has been strictly separated from the military in republican governments. The rationale for this deals with power and the fear of a centralized police force in a civil state. Unchecked police power is a threat to democracy; therefore, republican governments are very selective in the power delegated to police agencies. Law enforcement officers are given significant amounts of power in terms of regulating individual behavior, but little power in regulating whole social groups (Walker, 1977, introduction).

At this juncture the legal system intervenes. It dichotomizes civil police and military power, and it is the vehicle for regulating all forms of state authority. Military affairs are officially excluded from domestic enforcement duties while police power and legal authority exist in a symbiotic relationship within a "system" of justice. Domestic executive power may be utilized, but by the doctrine of *posse comitatus* it is separated from the power of war. Military force cannot be used to enforce civilian law. Further, the exercise of domestic power is inhibited by the restrictions in the Bill of Rights (Rotunda, 1987, p. 506). It is also interesting to note that these criteria do not forbid the police from defense operations.

The development of American law enforcement also helps to explain the current exercise of power. Models for American law enforcement came from the London Metropolitan Police of 1829. Robert Peel, then Home Secretary for the Conservative government, was faced with the problem of domestic unrest in industrializing British society. Small groups of police officers, such as the Bow Street Runners, had a solid record against crime and domestic unrest, but they were few in number and enjoyed no uniform rules for deployment. Generally, whether riot, strike, or street demonstration, one of the local British regiments was called to quell domestic disturbances. Faced with growing disruptions and crime, Peel created a civilian police force in 1829. It was completely segregated from the military, but based on a military hierarchy. (Johnson, 1981, pp. 17–35).

American police forces had begun to emerge on the East Coast a few years prior to Peel's reform movement. They, however, had lacked the cohesion of the London Metropolitan Police and, more importantly, had remained under local control with no standard idea of hierarchy and command (Lane, 1975, pp. 1–36). Gradually these forces evolved into large metropolitan agencies and used Peel's administrative model as their guide (Reppetto, 1978). As in Britain, the American police were structured in the mode of military forces, but they were strictly separated from military functions both by *posse comitatus* and local custom.

One aspect of policing remained clear, however. The police were not to be a military force. An interesting tradition of power sharing did emerge from emergency responses. While the Army was not used in domestic law enforcement, state National Guard units were used to augment police power (Holmes, 1971). The Bush administration has hinted at changes, suggesting military forces may be utilized for domestic law enforcement. This has created a storm of controversy. On the one hand, standard military logic as well as conventional wisdom would suggest that one should attack the enemy at his weakest link. In fact, Clausewitz (1984, Book 7, Chapter 15) urges this. The interesting aspect of American defense is that civilian domestic security forces may well represent the weakest link in the defense chain. On the other hand, strengthening this link with military force violates the Constitution (Dycus, 7-26-02). Historically, the police have no mandate for national defense, and military forces cannot be tasked with domestic law enforcement.

MANNING'S ANALYSIS
OF THE POLICE MANDATE

The major problem in the development of the American police centered on function. No one was sure what the police were supposed to do, and their operations varied from city to city. As society became more complex, the duties of the police grew in complexity. Unlike growing fire departments, the police had no single task. Peter Manning (1977, pp. 98–104) states that an occupational mandate refers to the professional right to claim expertise in a certain area. In the traditional professions, theologians, physicians, and attorneys all claim rights to a special body of knowledge beyond the comprehension of laymen. They are allowed to engage in specialized tasks and actions based on their expertise, in addition to exercising immense amounts of power within their fields. The mandate provides power, status, and justification. The American police enjoy no such mandate.

Manning (1977, pp. 127–138) argues that the police conform to their environment by using presentational strategies based on the social myth of law enforcement. The myth contends that police are set apart from society to control crime, and presentational strategies are used to externalize the myth; that is, the public is encouraged to accept the validity of the common assumption about policing. The problem in the process becomes apparent when the aspects of the myth are examined closely. The police are not set apart from society; they are a part of society. Further, and more damaging to the sacred aspects of the myth, the police cannot control crime. Since they respond without control, presentational strategies assume key importance.

According to Manning, presentational strategies involve attempts to satisfy a variety of external audiences through the manipulation of appearances. The police may not be able to control crime, but they can give the impression of doing so. This involves manipulating the way in which the police are viewed in the world outside the police departments. They actively encourage the "crime buster" image and claim to have abilities far beyond their realistic performance. Walker (1977, introduction) referred to this as the "heroic" image and argued that the police have portrayed this image of themselves throughout history.

The mandate is further confused by localization; that is, local political control and locally defined functions create a myriad of definitions of police work. As agencies compete for legitimacy by way of a mandate, American police forces find they must attempt to renew their legitimacy each day in a variety of manners. There is no single view of policing. Manning compares this to the situation in the United Kingdom where the law enforcement system had carved out its occupational niche and authority by the 1850s. While British police must compete with other agencies of social control for occupational space, their legitimacy is established. This is not so in America where the police are in a constant battle for legitimacy.

Given the local political orientation of the vast majority of American law enforcement agencies, the fear of crime in America, the struggle for legitimacy in police departments, and the presentational strategies of administrators, there were few incentives to pursue an effective policy of preparation for low level conflict prior to September 11. The sheer number of organizations, the overlapping jurisdictions, and the confusion about local, state, and federal roles lead to a morass of conflicting law enforcement purposes. With the exception of the FBI, American police agencies have not been given a mandate for national defense. This further confuses state and local responses to nebulous conflicts.

PATROL, INVESTIGATION, AND THE DEFENSE MISSION

The structure of modern warfare brings new responsibilities to civilian government. When the World Trade Center towers collapsed on American police officers, they became combatants in the shadow war of terrorism. This places two grave responsibilities in the hands of law enforcement. First, it is the responsibility of police to understand the nature of the conflict. Just as police are expected to handle emerging criminal or social problems, terrorism presents its own unique concerns. This is not to suggest that the majority of effort should be directed at defense, but it does suggest that role must be understood. Clear, mandated functions are necessary. Most importantly, the police should not be viewed as a reactive force. Because of their investigative and intelligence capabilities, they have the unique opportunity to strike terrorists before terrorists can attack.

Second, the defense role of the police is not a solitary function. On the one hand, law enforcement needs to develop policies, structures, and strategies that allow it to function as part of a civil defense team. It shares this role with fire and security services, emergency medical systems, and public health. On the other hand, relations and roles with National Guard and other military forces need to be clarified. Only law enforcement is in a position to take the lead in this arena. In other words, the police may develop an offensive role to prevent terrorist acts and defensive measures to react to destruction.

An analysis by *The Economist* (12-22-01, pp. 25–26) points to the problems of conceptualizing and mobilizing for homeland defense. President Bush created the Office of Homeland Security in October 2001. His purpose was to develop a comprehensive national strategy, but it did not emerge as expected. Congress presented more than 100 bills that dealt with security while the military sought to shore up weaknesses in the homeland.

Ironically, proactive measures in homeland defense immediately appeared from an unlikely area. *The Economist* highlights the Department of Justice's efforts to organize for a long term shadow war. American law enforcement may have a major role in the shadow war. It has the ability to gather information, networks to share intelligence, and, most importantly, the capability of taking offensive measures against terrorists before they strike. If state and local policymakers choose to accept a role in defense, it probably involves a return to the "eyes and ears" mission, a job surrounded by constitutional legalities and bureaucratic realities. If accepted, domestic intelligence systems, once abused, must be revamped and operated under the norms of democratic control. In addition, state and local law enforcement agencies need to have a method for sharing intelligence with agencies traditionally aimed at national defense. There are policies and procedures to develop, formal and informal relationships to cultivate.

STATE AND LOCAL POLICE
AND INTERNATIONAL AFFAIRS

When considering the nature of asymmetrical warfare, it is possible to argue that America has been involved in an emergency situation for quite some time. The shadow war began with attacks against diplomatic targets in the Middle East and increased in both intensity and lethality. State and local law officers gradually became part of the process as America's enemies grew strong enough to launch attacks on U.S. soil. When a group of violent religious extremists sought to topple the World Trade Center in 1993, they failed. On September 11, 2001, their allies succeeded.

Although any date is subjective, one might say that the current struggle started around 1979 in the midst of the Iranian revolution. Shiite Revolutionary Guards seized the American embassy in Tehran, and the United States was unable to do anything about it. The lessons of asymmetry were clear to our enemies. A weak power could strike the United States because Americans were reluctant to go to war. As the years went on, attacks increased (see Wright, 1986 and 1989).

In 1982 Israel invaded Lebanon, allegedly to stop Palestine Liberation Organization (PLO) attacks from the south. The war went far beyond the original publicly stated objectives of the Israelis, and the region soon bogged down in a savage conflict involving massacres, terrorism, and—for the first time in the area—suicide bombings. Iran's Revolutionary Guards entered the fray, and the United States joined a multinational peace-keeping force. To the opponents of Israel, however, the presence of American forces seemed to be anything but that of neutral peacekeepers. The Party of God, Hezbollah, began a terrorist campaign to remove the American forces. Between 1983 and 1989 Hezbollah bombed the American embassy in Beirut; killed top CIA operations officers in another bombing; kidnapped several Americans in Lebanon, executing two of them; and destroyed the Marine barracks in Beirut. The United States was unable to respond effectively. Asymmetry again appeared to be working as the world's leading military power was held at bay.

Lessons from this experience were reinforced when forces from the former Soviet Union left Afghanistan in 1989. For violent religious extremists, Soviet defeat translated into holy victory. If holy warriors, the mujahideen reasoned, could beat the Soviets, they could beat anyone. Former mujahideen fighters gravitated to one of their leaders, Osama bin Laden, to begin a campaign against the United States. Bin Laden and his advisors were well aware of Hezbollah's success against the United States in Lebanon (PBS, 2001b).

As America's enemies began to wage asymmetrical war, many Americans, even those in the highest places, sometimes failed to grasp the significance and the nature of the shadow war. Osama bin Laden wasn't even on the American radar screen in 1996 (Bergen, 2001, pp. 64–67). Regardless, America had been in the sights of Islamic radicals for a number of years and bin Laden became a symbolic focal point for aiming those sights. His attacks would eventually involve American law enforcement. (See Box 4.4)

PBS (2001a and 2001b) dates the beginning of al Qaeda's campaign as December 29, 1992, when two terrorists tried to kill American servicemen in Yemen, soldiers who were detailed for duty in Somalia. Two months later, radicals tried to topple the World Trade Center. One of the participants, Ramzi Youseff, struck again in 1995, only to be thwarted by Philippine police. In an operation code named Operation Bojinka, Youseff hoped to assassinate the Pope and bring down eleven airliners over the Pacific.

Bin Laden and his associates had global aspirations. Back in Somalia in October 1993, Islamic militants downed an American helicopter, spawning a day-long battle in Mogadishu. Bin Laden claimed he trained the forces that struck the American forces. Bombing attacks in 1995 and 1996 targeted U.S. forces in Saudi Arabia. Although there was no direct link to al Qaeda, the bombers had sympathy with bin Laden's cause. Two deadly bombs killed hundreds on August 7, 1998, as al Qaeda struck the American embassies in Dar es Salaam, Tanzania, and Nairobi, Kenya. Suicide bombers hit the USS *Cole* on October 12, 2000. The largest al Qaeda attack came on September 11, 2001, in New York and Washington, DC.

CLAUSEWITZ, SUN TZU, AND ASYMMETRY

Clausewitz, Sun Tzu, and asymmetry are not standard topics in either theoretical criminology cousrses or pragmatic police training programs, and preventative patrol and investigative methods are based in state and local police departments, not the Department of Defense. Yet, the nature of modern international terrorism has thrown American police agencies into the darkness of a shadow war. State and local law enforcement will be called to protect the public, respond to emergencies, and investigate attacks. If they plan for the protection of civil liberties and the realities of interagency bureaucratic relations, they may be able

---

BOX 4.4   Close-Up: Al Qaeda's Campaign of Terror

12-29-92	Aden, Yemen	Hotel bombing
2-26-93	New York City	First World Trade Center bombing
10-3-93	Mogadishu, Somalia	Firefight U.S. Army Rangers
Late 1994	Manila, Philippines	Operation Bojinka
12-26-95	Addo Abada, Ethiopia	Attempted assassination of Hosni Mubarak
11-13-95	Riyadh, Saudi Arabia	Car bomb U.S. military personnel*
6-25-96	Dharan, Saudi Arabia	Truck bomb U.S. Air Force base*
8-7-98	Dar es Salaam, Tanzania	U.S. Embassy bombing
8-7-98	Nairobi, Kenya	U.S. Embassy bombing
12-4-99	Port Angeles, Washington	Foiled bombing plot
December 1999	Amman, Jordan	Foiled bombing plot
10-12-00	Aden, Yemen	Boat bomb USS *Cole*
12-25-00	Strasbourg, France	Foiled bombing plot
9-11-01	New York City	World Trade Center attacks
9-11-01	Washington, DC	Pentagon attack
9-11-01	Pennsylvania	Attack foiled by hijack victims
9-13-01	Paris, France	Foiled bombing plot
9-13-01	Brussels, Belgium	Foiled bombing plot
9-19-01	Detroit, Michigan	Alleged sleeper cell closed
10-8-01	Sarajevo, Bosnia	Foiled attack
October 2001	Madrid, Spain	Sleeper cell closed
Early 2002	Singapore	Three sleeper cells closed
4-11-02	Djerba, Tunisia	Truck bombing of a synagogue
Summer 2002	Gibraltar	Foiled naval attack
Summer 2002	West Coast, United States	Alleged Sleeper cell closed
Fall 2002	New York	Alleged Sleeper cell closed
10-6-02	Aden, Yemen	Boat bomb, French merchant ship
10-9-02	Kuwait	Marines attacked by two gunmen
10-12-02	Bali, Indonesia	Bombing of a nightclub
11-12-02	Unknown	Tape claiming to be bin Laden praises recent violence

*The FBI has not established links between al Qaeda and this attack. These attacks may be linked to Hezbollah or similar group.

SOURCES: *Time* Magazine, *PBS Frontline*, *Detroit Free Press*, *New York Times.*

to conduct effective offensive and defensive operations. If they overreact, individual freedom may be jeopardized, and civilian police agencies may take on a militaristic attitude.

America's police have been called to homeland security because the nature of conflict is changing. Technology and communications provide the base for asymmetrical war, but law enforcement lacks an occupational mandate for national defense. It could even be argued that the police have little to do with the mobilization of national will in the type of war described by Clausewitz. Yet, the police are now faced with low-level political conflicts, both foreign and domestic, both political and psychological. America's law enforcement agencies have responded to school shootings, domestic extremist bombings, foreign suicide attacks, and communities held in terror by random serial killers in the past decade. Conflict is changing and homeland security will require state and local law enforcement agencies to rethink the Clausewitzian paradigm. It is not a question of whether America is at war or at peace, the issue centers on the willingness of state and local agencies to develop new skills for national security. If police agencies are to play a role in defense, it is time to move beyond Clausewitz.

5

Taking the Offense

The United States experienced international terrorism in two distinct waves from 1983 to the present. Driven by the 1979 Shiite revolution in Iran and the subsequent takeover of the American Embassy in Tehran, America encountered suicide bombings and kidnappings in Lebanon from 1983 to 1989. Shiite violence intermingled with secular attacks by Libya and the Abu Nidal Organization. America responded by launching military raids in Libya and Lebanon, arresting terrorists in foreign lands, imposing economic sanctions, and developing a list of states supporting terrorism. By 1992 the rules had changed. The new international enemy was Sunni extremism coming not only from the Middle East, but also from Central Asia and North Africa. With attacks on the American homeland, the new wave of violence brought international terrorism to the doorstep of U.S. police agencies. If state and local police agencies choose to tackle the problem, they need proactive tactics. In other words, the most effective actions in the shadow war will take the fight to the enemy and not merely wait for the enemy to attack. Intelligence gathering and information sharing are the keys to offensive action.

After reading this chapter, you should be able to

1. List four questions to guide offensive operations against terrorists.

2. Define the advantages of proactive preparations over reactive responses.

3. Summarize Bodrero's three-part model for proactive operations.

4. Cite the differences between criminal and terrorist behavior.

5. Summarize topics for counterterrorist training.

6. Describe a method for building an intelligence system in local police departments.

7. Outline issues involved in proactive counterterrorist planning.

8. Explain the importance of sharing information.

9. Describe why proactive intelligence systems will eventually fail.

QUESTIONS TO SET THE OFFENSE

Imagine the following scene: On a snowy afternoon a road patrol deputy stops a car on a Nebraska highway. Everything looks routine and the driver, a foreign national, is exceedingly polite. The deputy notices that the car is registered in South Carolina and that the driver has an operator's permit issued in Colorado. The deputy asks questions about the driver's country of origin, his South Carolina or Colorado residence, and his reason for driving through Nebraska. The answers are smooth, as if they have been rehearsed. When the deputy uses nuances to allow the driver to answer in a different manner, the driver reverts to seemingly rehearsed answers.

In the course of questioning, the deputy finds that the car is rented, and the driver's name is spelled one way on his license and another way on the rental agreement. Further questioning reveals immigration papers with a third spelling. At this point, the deputy begins to ask more in-depth questions. The deputy knows multiple spellings of names and mastering false identification are subjects mastered by many international terrorists. Perhaps the deputy has encountered nothing at all, or perhaps there is more evidence underneath the surface. It is possible to uncover terrorist activity, or any other type of crime, by aggressively following suspicions.

The foregoing example is only imaginary, but recently a Midwestern police officer stopped a vehicle on an interstate highway for speeding. The car contained two men and a number of other items, objects that failed to attract the officer's attention. The patrol officer failed to notice a cache of weapons and explosives in the car, two loaded automatic weapons behind the driver, and a semiautomatic pistol by the driver's hand. He also missed violent racist literature and other extremist propaganda lying open in the car. He failed to see the clue that should have given warning when he first approached the car, a Ku Klux Klan symbol on the back window. Failing to do a proper warrant check, he did not know that one of the men was a fugitive. He gave the driver a speeding ticket never knowing that his life had been in danger or that the men in the car were planning to bomb a Fourth of July celebration (Keathley, 2002).

A Missouri state trooper reported the details of the stop later. The trooper, who knew one of the men in the car, said that the two occupants in the stopped vehicle had had a conversation about killing the unobservant police officer. The man the trooper knew was a committed, violent right-wing extremist with a criminal history and an outstanding warrant. The extremist belonged to a Christian identity group hoping to set off a bomb in Texas that would dwarf Timothy McVeigh's 1995 Oklahoma City truck bomb. Killing a police officer was an accepted course of action in his campaign against the government. The reason the Missouri trooper knew so much about the attitude and beliefs of the extremist was that he was also in the car working undercover (Keathley, 2002).

In another incident, a West Virginia state trooper stopped a van full of bootleg cigarettes, thinking he had uncovered a cigarette scheme. Such schemes are criminally profitable due to varying state tobacco laws and tax systems. In this case the suspects purchased cigarettes in North Carolina and ran them to Michigan. North Carolina had a five cent tax per pack on the cigarettes and a fifty cent charge per carton. Michigan, however, taxed cigarettes at seventy-five cents per pack and $7.50 per carton. North Carolina did not require a tax stamp, but Michigan did. Smugglers ran cigarettes from North Carolina to Michigan, stamped them with Michigan tax stamps, and sold them at regular prices without paying taxes. In this case, the trooper reported the stop to the ATF, but the ATF agents were not surprised by the discovery. They had been working on the case with a sheriff's department in North Carolina.

The U.S. Attorney for western North Carolina, Robert Conrad, began investigating the case, assuming the suspects were smuggling North Carolina cigarettes to Michigan and profiting by not paying tax. This turned out to be the base of the investigation, as the smugglers kept some of the money, but other illegal profits took a strange path. Conrad followed some money to Vancouver, Canada, and other profits went overseas. Conrad's office and ATF investigators traced the money to Lebanon. Far from a simple cigarette scheme, the smuggling operation turned out to be an operation to support Hezbollah, a Shiite terrorist group based in Lebanon (*United States v. Mohamad Hammoud,* 2002). The Charlotte Hezbollah Cell, as it came to be known, was broken because investigators and prosecutors looked beyond the surface.

If state and local police agencies are to take a proactive stance against terrorism, law enforcement personnel will need to factor counterterrorist issues into everyday police situations. Albeit in a military report, the Department of Defense (DOD) identifies those factors in an examination of the USS *Cole* in Aden, Yemen, in October 2000 (DOD, 1-9-01). The investigative committee discusses issues applicable to all security forces, including local law enforcement. Its primary focus is to identify the best tool police agencies can use against terrorism: intelligence.

The DOD report calls for an offensive strategy against terror networks; in military vernacular it recommends "force protection." The civilian world of law enforcement refers to the same concept as "security," but the DOD findings are as applicable to civil society as they are to military situations. The report urges American forces to develop abilities to detect and disrupt terrorists before they can launch operations. The key to offensive action, the DOD report states, is increased intelligence. If units assigned to force protection gather information and share it, the report concludes, it may be possible to disrupt terror attacks.

Although it is a military report, it presents sound policy for state and local law enforcement. It is as relevant to military units assigned to force protection as it is to stopping white supremacists in the Midwest or Hezbollah in Charlotte.

A congressional report issued two years earlier arrives at a similar conclusion (Perl, 1998). Terrorism, Perl argues, represents a significant portion of future conflict. America needs to become more aggressive and disrupt terrorists before they can strike U.S. interests. International terrorists have increasingly targeted the United States, Perl states, and attacks in the homeland are inevitable. The shift in international terrorism demands a changing offensive strategy. Perl includes a set of pointed questions, tempering calls for increased intelligence with concern for the Constitution, law, and civil liberties. Before beginning proactive operations, Perl says policymakers need to ask:

How should America prepare for undeclared war?

How should the legislative and executive branches interact?

How could public support be maintained over extended periods of time?

How could American civil liberties be protected while fighting terrorism?

These questions suggest issues and policies for state and local law enforcement.

Police officers will encounter terrorists in the same manner they come across criminals. Preparation for a shadow war involves recognition of issues and the skills to act as an extension of the communities being protected. Beyond practical skills, proactive policies need to take shape within the bounds of the Constitution. If the police do not act to protect civil liberties, offensive strategies will undermine the very society the agencies have sworn to protect.

OVERCOMING REACTION

American law enforcement has a long tradition of reactive patrol. With the advent of radio-dispatched motorized patrol, response time became the measure of police effectiveness. The assumption behind the theory was the sooner police arrived at the scene of a crime, the more likely they were to make an arrest. Like fire departments responding to smoke, police effectiveness was determined by its ability to respond to crime.

The problem of terrorism brings the need for preemptive policing to a new level. If law enforcement simply responds, it will have little impact on the prevention of terrorism. Defensive reaction alone leaves the initiative with terrorist organizations. In addition, no government can afford to fortify all the potential targets in a jurisdiction. Even if all targets could be defended, the goal of asymmetrical warfare is not to destroy targets, but to show that security forces are not in charge. Terrorists are free to strike the least-defended symbolic target. Defensive thinking, like reactive patrol, cannot win a shadow war.

If state and local agencies shift to offensive thinking and action, two results will inevitably develop. First, police contact with potential terrorists will increase, but as Sherry Colb (10-10-01) points out, the vast majority of any ethnic or social group is made up of people who abhor terrorism. This increases the possibility of negative stereotyping and the abuse of power. Second, proactive measures demand increased intelligence and much of the information will have no relation to criminal activity. If not properly monitored, such intelligence may be misused.

Another issue appears in the private sector. Kayyem and Howitt (2002) find that offensive action begins in the local community. To illustrate this, note that both the hypothetical and real life examples of counterterrorism used in this chapter were initiated by local agencies. The weakness in local systems occurs, however, because state and local police departments do not frequently think beyond their jurisdictions, and they do not routinely take advantage of potential partnerships inside their bailiwicks. Kayyem and Howitt believe partnerships are the key to community planning. One of the greatest potential allies is private security. Unfortunately, many law enforcement agencies frown upon private security and fail to create joint ventures with the private sector.

On the positive side of the debate, counterterrorism is not a mystical operation. It uses many of the skills already employed in preventative patrol, criminal investigation, and surveillance. With a few tweaks, police intelligence operations and drug enforcement units can add counterterrorism to their agendas, and patrol and investigative units can be trained to look for terrorist activities in the course of their normal duties. If properly managed, these activities need not present a threat to civil liberties. D. Douglas Bodrero, Utah's former commissioner for criminal justice and long-standing member of the International Association of Chiefs of Police (IACP) terrorism committee, has proposed a proactive model for state and local counterterrorist action.

BODRERO'S MODEL

D. Douglas Bodrero (2002) examines the proactive police role in the post–September 11 environment. The mission for state and local law enforcement after the September terrorist attacks is the same as it has always been, to protect life and property. After September 11, the Department of Justice made combating terrorism one of its top priorities, Bodrero argues, and the FBI began reorganizing in late 2001 with increased emphasis on counterterrorism, counterintelligence, and cybercrime. No one is better equipped to take the offensive, in Bodrero's mind, than state and local law enforcement because no agency is closer to the community than its local police. He foresees a partnership between local departments and the FBI.

Mirroring the federal government's approach to counterterrorism, Bodrero argues there are three distinct responses to terrorism: interdiction and prevention, crisis management, and consequence management. Comprised of skills honed during criminal investigations and intelligence operations, interdiction and prevention become the essence of offensive action. They alone allow law enforcement to strike before the terrorists. Crisis management refers to controlling an incident while it is in progress, while consequence management is designed to respond to terrorism after the fact. Consequence management is emergency response, and it falls in the domain of "first responders." In reality, the differences between crisis and consequence management are minimal, and all first responders are reacting to incidents (see Cilluffo et al., 2001 and Commission on National Security, 2001). Police officers are proactive when they intercept terrorists before an incident. Bodrero believes interdiction and prevention should be the main goals of law enforcement.

Bodrero states that interdiction and prevention measures are composed of three primary activities: training for recognition and procedures, constructing and using intelligence systems, and planning for counterterrorism. Line officers need training in counterterrorism. They need to know what to look for, how to gather information, and how to feed information through analytical systems. It is not enough to train. Agencies must work to build structures to gather, sort, and analyze information, and analysis is particularly important. All of the information in the world will not combat terrorism unless decision makers know what it means. Analyzing information is the key to success, even when the analysis of some information is little more than educated guesswork. Information must also be shared. If it sits in one agency, it does little good. This is a challenge for police officers, who live in a world of secrecy. Finally, to make this system work, Bodrero says, administrators must develop comprehensive plans. Planning for emergencies completes the proactive process of counterterrorism. If Bodrero is correct, all three issues deserve further examination.

Training

Training is the starting point for counterterrorist operations. It does no good to talk about offensive actions if officers do not understand the problem. Operational training should be focused on patrol and nonspecialized investigations. Specialized investigative units, such as undercover operations and drug enforcement, should receive advanced training because they are in a unique position to gather criminal intelligence. Since terrorists conduct themselves differently than common criminals, detectives and other investigators need to understand terrorist behavior. Patrol officers, in particular, need to develop abilities to recognize potential terrorist situations during routine field contacts, and administrators need to manage the complexity of multiagency systems designed to share information.

The Bureau of Justice Assistance developed the State and Local Anti-Terrorism Training (SLATT) program shortly after the Oklahoma City bombing in 1995. It contains general information for operational personnel, specialized investigative training, and executive workshops. Some of the SLATT offerings also focus on interagency relations, FBI cooperation with local departments, and civil liberties. In late 2002, SLATT began a nationwide program to train anti-terrorism instructors for police agencies. The SLATT program could easily serve as a model for initiating a comprehensive national training program for state and local police agencies.

Recent incidents indicate the importance of recognition for operational personnel. In December 1994 local police officers in the Philippines were called to an apartment fire. Upon arrival they found laboratory equipment similar to the type used in illegal drug labs. Resisting the impulse to confiscate or destroy the equipment and make arrests, the police probed further. Their actions saved hundreds, maybe thousands, of lives. The apartment belonged to Ramzi Youseff, one of the conspirators in the 1993 World Trade Center bombing. The police had unwittingly uncovered a plot Youseff called "Operation Bojinka." An operative for Osama bin Laden's al Qaeda network, Youseff planned to bring down a dozen American passenger planes over the Pacific Ocean and to assassinate the Pope. His apartment contained bomb-making equipment and detailed records stored on a computer. The local police conducted a thorough investigation and turned the evidence over to American police officials. Their actions stopped a disaster (PBS, 2001b and Elliot, 11-12-01).

America has experienced similar situations more directly. William Ferrell (1990) summarizes the routine traffic stop of a New Jersey state trooper in 1988. The alert trooper became suspicious after observing a man, Yu Kikumura, in a rest stop along the New Jersey turnpike. After stopping the car and investigating, the trooper found bomb-making materials in Kikumura's car. Further investigation revealed that Kikumura was a member of the Japanese Red Army on a mission to bomb American targets.

Another incident involves an alert customs officer who prevented a disaster through aggressive patrol work in December 1999 (Bower, 11-12-01 and White, 2003). At Port Angeles in Washington State, the officer became suspicious when an overly nervous person attempted to pass through customs. She pressed questions, causing the man to blunder. The alert customs agent had uncovered Ahmed Rassad, an al Qaeda terrorist, on his way to the Los Angeles airport with bomb-making equipment. When questioned, Rassad became an intelligence gold mine, divulging a plethora of information about the al Qaeda network.

Counterterrorist training for the patrol and investigative services should be aimed at general recognition. In other words, officers should learn to recognize the "who, what, where, and how" of terrorist groups and ideologies operating in the United States. Just as officers recognize behavioral characteristics associated with robbery and burglary, so must they become familiar with terrorist behavior. In April 1995 an observant Oklahoma state trooper stopped Timothy McVeigh for a traffic violation. Operating with knowledge of general information hastily assembled by investigators, the trooper knew enough to question and detain McVeigh, eventually capturing the homegrown terrorist through routine police work. Counterterrorism begins with patrol. Basic recognition of terrorism is one of the keys to counterterrorism, and it should become the core of general training. (See Box 5.1.)

Recognition can develop when one understands the behavior of terrorists as compared to common criminals. Bodrero (2002) believes common street criminals and terrorists have differing values, motivations, and criminological behavior patterns. To begin with, common street criminals are opportunistic. They take action when a target is vulnerable, and many times they are under

---

**BOX 5.1   Close-Up: Differences between Terrorists
and Common Criminals**

Terrorists are:	*Common Criminals are:*
Teleological, following a purpose	Opportunistic
Committed to a cause	Uncommitted
Oriented to a group or cause	Self-centered
Disciplined	Undisciplined
Trained	Untrained
Target or attack oriented	Escape oriented

SOURCE: *The Police Chief,* February 2002.

---

the influence of drugs or alcohol when committing a crime. Professional criminals may plan crimes, but prisons are filled with street criminals who do not. Most police action is devoted to street criminals. By contrast, terrorists plan extensively, conducting reconnaissance of targets and employing a variety of counterintelligence operations to avoid detection. Sulc (1996, p. 28) points out that terrorists even infiltrate police agencies to thwart law enforcement. The teleological orientation of terrorists differs from a common criminal's desire for immediate gratification.

There are other differences. Teleological orientation brings commitment. Bodrero (2002) argues that terrorists are committed to, indeed consumed by, their cause. They are violent true believers, many times on a holy mission, focused on an objective. On the other hand, common criminals are not devoted to crime; they are interested in their own satisfaction. While terrorists train, sometimes for years, to achieve objectives, street criminals take immediate action with the resources at hand. The goal of a terrorist is to strike the target at any cost. The goal of a street criminal is to hit the easiest target and run. Terrorists will stand and fight police officers; in many cases they will even initiate attacks. Street criminals often stand and fight, but their purpose is to escape.

Information obtained from al Qaeda training camps (Fineman and Braun, 9-24-01) illustrates the point. Osama bin Laden's training philosophy involved three tiers and multiple weeks of training. On the basic level, recruits received guerrilla training. Painstakingly translated into Arabic, many al Qaeda training pamphlets from guerrilla sites were taken from U.S. military manuals and paramilitary publications. The second tier aimed at preparing terrorists. It included detailed preparation in bomb making, weapons, and tactics. Some terrorists trained for more than a year, and they kept records so that groups could be managed. The third tier focused on managerial schools in cell administration for selected terrorists. These schools offered "graduate-level" training for the best terrorists. Street criminals do not meticulously prepare for a life of crime.

Retired FBI agent William Dyson (2002) analyzes terrorist preparation with a humorous illustration. It is impossible to picture, Dyson says, a gang member or associate of an organized crime family preparing for work in a manner similar to a terrorist. Imagine, Dyson exclaims, a member of the Mafia devoting years researching the theory of crime! A professional criminal might read a book or two or even train with a mentor, but criminals are not consumed with an ideology. Criminals are motivated by personal gain. Terrorists, in juxtaposition, are totally dedicated to a cause. They immerse themselves in ideology and pragmatic action, and this becomes their way of life.

In contrast to these arguments, it is not possible to suggest that there is a psychological profile of "the terrorist personality" or a behavioral description of a common terrorist (Laqueur, 1999, pp. 79–104; and Ross 1999, pp. 169–192). Terrorism fluctuates in response to differing social and political circumstances. Some analysts, such as Walter Laqueur, believe it is impossible to model terrorist behavior. Others, like Jeffery Ross, offer a more promising view, but they maintain that a variety of political and social factors must be individually applied to terrorist cases. Terrorists are unlike common criminals, but such recognition is not the beginning of a behavioral model. It is to be used as an indicator to alert police officers.

Having said this, there is a second danger. If officers are trained to recognize the characteristics of true believers, it may spawn investigations of political activity. Dyson (2002) summarizes it well, stating that all terrorists are true believers, but not all true believers are terrorists. (A true believer is consumed by a cause and sees little else in life.) Robert Taylor (2002) says the danger of proactive police counterterrorist measures is law enforcement officers may cross the line from investigating violent activity to intelligence gathering about political action. Taylor believes that many of the Bush administration's proposed police powers will not survive court scrutiny. While this section advocates training in the recognition of terrorism, it is important once again to stress caution. A system that destroys civil liberties is unacceptable to most Americans.

Training state and local officers to recognize problem behavior is the first step in preparing for terrorism because many officers misinterpret the problem. For example, consider a sampling of comments my colleagues and I have heard in anti-terrorist training sessions around the United States:

- A command officer from the South was surprised to find that antigovernment extremists were driving cars bearing homemade "constitutional" license plates.
- A sheriff from New England handled a malicious destruction of property complaint not knowing the victim had been attacked by an ecoterrorist.
- A state police lieutenant described armed white supremacists in his state as "law-abiding friends and neighbors."
- Many state and local officers did not know that Abu Nidal operated in Missouri and Tennessee and that the framework for Hamas appeared in Michigan.
- Police officers perpetually worry when they see a mosque, inappropriately assuming Islam is a violent religion.

These examples demonstrate the importance of recognition. Training is a necessary first step, but it must be complemented with law enforcement management structures dedicated to the protection of individual rights and judicial oversight to prevent abuses in intelligence gathering.

Building Intelligence Systems

Information gathering is akin to academic research. Before beginning, a researcher needs basic knowledge of a field and an understanding of subdisciplines. Much of this background information has no direct bearing on the actual question a researcher is trying to answer, but without background preparation, the researcher cannot address the question. Command of basic information allows the researcher to move toward applying results. Applied information, the specificity the researcher seeks, is divided into both in-depth knowledge about a specific topic and the latest information from the discipline. In the sciences and social sciences, this process leads a researcher from general concepts to applied ideas, from abstract principles to glimpses of reality. While academic in nature, this process is directly applicable to gathering intelligence. Police intelligence systems can be modeled after academic research. Basic intelligence involves general information about a subject and its subdisciplines. Applied intelligence involves gathering basic information about a target and real-time information about current activities.

The practical application of this process comes through organizing structures aimed at collecting, analyzing, and forwarding information. Someone in every American law enforcement agency should be assigned to collect and forward terrorist intelligence. In small agencies this may mean assigning a person who represents several police and sheriffs departments, while in moderate-sized agencies the function could be performed in the detective bureau or the planning unit. Large metropolitan and state police agencies need full-time intelligence units. At the state and regional level, efforts must be made to assemble, categorize, and analyze information and place it within a national and international context.

Law enforcement and national defense intelligence came under difficult times during the administration of President Jimmy Carter (1976–1980). Carter was not seeking to dismantle intelligence operations; he wanted to protect Americans from their government. The President tried to correct the abuse of power and end the scandal of using covert operations against American citizens. The CIA had tested drugs and biological agents on unknowing citizens, while the FBI's counterintelligence program (COINTELPRO) exceeded the authority of law enforcement. In responding to such abuses, the government began to limit the power of intelligence operations, unintentionally hampering their effectiveness.

President Carter's reaction was understandable, but critics believe he went too far and no other administration has been able to reconstitute effective intelligence organizations. A *Time* magazine article (Calabresi and Ratnesar, 3-11-02) states the issue succinctly: America needs to learn to spy

BOX 5.2 Close-Up: Tips for Building an Intelligence System

Copy Models that Work—Look at other agencies and systems. The California Anti-Terrorism Information Center (CATIC) and New Jersey State Police Intelligence Service Section, for example, have systems that might well serve as a model for the nation.

Take Advantage of Current Information Systems—Some states and regions already have information-sharing systems. The Regional Information Sharing System (RISS) is such an organization; it is a secure network, and it is controlled by state and local law enforcement.

Use Internet Mining and Other Information-Gathering Techniques—Services that routinely gather information help to place localized structures in the big picture.

Teach Patrol Officers and Investigators—Deputies, troopers, and patrol officers can become the eyes and ears of a national intelligence system. To be effective, they must know what to look for.

Develop a System for Reporting and Forwarding—If patrol information remains localized, it is not optimally effective. It must be categorized, analyzed, and shared.

Accept Excess Results—A good intelligence-gathering system will produce more information than agencies can use. This is the nature of intelligence. Excess information is not wasteful.

Plan for Failure—Even the best systems cannot catch everything. Eventually, terrorists will strike. When this happens, good reaction plans are a necessity.

again. Law enforcement has a role, the *Time* authors argue, and human intelligence must be increased. The journalists adamantly censure bureaucratic structures for failing to share information, and they condemn the system for relying too heavily on machine and electronic information. Another weak point, the writers state, is the inability to analyze information. Intelligence is fragmented and ineffective. Their opinion has been reflected in both the academic and intelligence communities (Best, 12-3-01; Betts, 2002; and Wise, 6-2-02).

Despite the limitations on intelligence gathering, it is possible for law enforcement agencies to gather information, store it in an analytical database, and share it with other officers. Patty Dobbs-Medaris (2002) demonstrates that agencies receiving federal money are allowed to collect criminal intelligence. As long as agencies reasonably suspect criminal activity, she says, law enforcement agencies may gather and store criminal intelligence. The Patriot Act increases the ability of law enforcement and intelligence agencies to share information, but David Carter, one of the foremost academic experts on law enforcement intelligence in the country, solemnly warns that the abuses of the past cannot be repeated if police agencies want to develop effective intelligence systems (Dreyfuss, 3-23-02). (See Box 5.2.)

Not only is it possible to build intelligence systems within the letter and spirit of legal regulations, several agencies have an excellent track record in doing so. The New Jersey State Police (NJSP), for example, have an extensive intelligence-gathering apparatus (New Jersey State Police, 2002). The NJSP Intelligence Service Section is made up of three main divisions. The Intelligence Bureau is the largest division, composed of six units. The Analytical Unit is responsible for reviewing data from organized crime families and street gangs. It synthesizes information to produce a broad picture of the entire state, and it is also used to conduct threat assessments for major public events. The Casino Intelligence Unit collects information on gambling affiliations with traditional and nontraditional crimes. It also serves as the government's liaison for regulatory agencies and conducts background investigations on contractors working in the casino industry. The Electronic Surveillance Unit conducts court-authorized monitoring and assists federal agencies in national security investigations. Critical information is shared through the Liaison Computerized Services Unit, including the sharing of information with agencies outside New Jersey. The Services Unit also codifies and organizes intelligence reports. Finally, the Street Gang Unit collects information and works with local gang task forces. The NJSP system is a model for gathering, organizing, analyzing, and sharing criminal information.

Two other divisions complete the picture for the NJSP system, including a unit for terrorist intelligence. The Central Security Unit is responsible for New Jersey's counterterrorist mission. Its primary purpose is the prevention of terrorist activities through intelligence operations. In other words, it is a proactive organization designed to prevent terrorism through interdiction. According to its official public statement, the Central Security Unit is primarily concerned with civil peace, protecting dignitaries, and monitoring known hate groups. The Solid Waste Unit, gathering information about hazardous materials as well as keeping an eye on organized crime, and the Casino Bureau round out the organization of the NJSP Intelligence Service Section. The key to its organization, and its preventative capabilities, is the collection, analysis, and sharing of information. Recently, NJSP linked its intelligence service with federal law enforcement, giving it the potential for greater effectiveness. (See Box 5.3)

Recently, the state of California has introduced a new concept in statewide intelligence systems, the California Anti-Terrorism Information Center (CATIC). Formed after September 11, California created a statewide intelligence system designed to combat terrorism. Dividing operational zones into five administrative areas, it links federal, state, and local information services in one system. Trained intelligence analysts operate within civil rights guidelines and utilize information in a secure communications system (California Department of Justice, 2001). Information is analyzed daily.

CATIC is quite unique in state and local law enforcement. It combines both machine intelligence with information coming from a variety of police agencies. The information is correlated and organized by analysts looking for trends. Future projections are made by looking at past indicators. Rather than simply operating as an information gathering unit, CATIC is a synthesizing process. It combines open-source public information with criminal trends and possible terrorist activities. Processed intelligence is designed to produce threat assessments for each area and to project trends outside the jurisdiction. In other

---

BOX 5.3   Close-Up: The New Jersey Intelligence System

The New Jersey State Police Web site says its intelligence activities are designed to

- Assist law enforcement agencies in combating organized crime and terrorism.
- Share information with other agencies.
- Process requests from other law enforcement agencies.

- Participate outside jurisdictional boundaries through the Middle Atlantic Great Lakes Organized Crime Law Enforcement Network (MAGLOCLEN) and International Criminal Police Organization (INTERPOL).
- Maintain information security.

SOURCE: New Jersey State Police.

---

words, CATIC attempts to process multiple sources of information to predict threats. By centralizing the collection and analytical sections of a statewide system, California's Department of Justice may have developed a method for moving offensively against terrorism.

The New York City Police Department has taken the offensive spirit a step further. Police Commissioner Raymond Kelly created two new units, one for counterterrorism and one for intelligence. Retired Marine Corps General Frank Libutti heads the counterterrorism section, while a former high-ranking CIA official, David Cohen, was selected to head the intelligence section. Kelly stated that he wanted the NYPD to do a better job of intelligence analysis and to work more closely with the federal government. The International Association of Chiefs of Police (IACP) said the plan was appropriate for New York City (Johnson, 1-29-02).

While the official versions of law enforcement intelligence systems suggest that the police are on the offensive, others look below the surface. The FBI and CIA have been criticized resoundingly for failing to gather information prior to the September 11 attacks and ineffectively analyzing the information they did have (Dillon, 10-4-01 and Nordland, Yousafzi, and Dehghanpisheh, 8-19-02). The Bush administration and police agencies expressed disapproval of the FBI's information-sharing policies (Fields, 5-3-02). Civil liberties groups fear growing power in agencies associated with homeland security, while others express concern over expanding executive authority (Herman, 12-3-01). Finally, David Carter's (Dreyfuss, 3-23-02) warning about the abuse of intelligence units cannot be ignored.

Public bureaucracies are sometimes adept at explaining the ideal while making few changes. Two classic studies of bureaucracy illustrate the point. Donald P. Warwick (1975) examines change inside the Department of State, concluding that stagnation and ineffectiveness characterize the State Department despite the best efforts to introduce reforms. Anthony C. Downs (1967) argues that bureaucratic inertia cancels the ability of reforming zealots to introduce

---

BOX 5.4   Close-Up: Basic Planning for Terrorism

Information for Planning
- List threats and possible targets
- List available resources
- Project potential attacks
- Identify critical infrastructures

Factors Influencing Plans
- Emergency command structures
- Coordination among agencies

- Mass casualties
- Victim and family support
- Preservation of evidence
- Crime scene management
- Media relations
- Costs
- Training and preincident exercises

SOURCE: International Association of Chiefs of Police, 2001.

---

change to organizations. Newer studies point to the key for positive change. When an organization has dynamic interaction with its environment, it can deal effectively with problems (Swanson, Territo, and Taylor, 2001, pp. 136–164). The New Jersey State Police intelligence unit and California's CATIC plans may well overcome concerns and bureaucratic problems. The proof will come if they continue to follow through with current plans, offering protection from terrorists and protection of civil liberties.

Planning

Two of the most well-respected scholars in criminal justice planning are John Hudzik and Gary Cordner. Hudzik and Cordner (1983) argue that planning should take place prior to the emergence of a problem. Effective police planning incorporates a description of a goal and methods for achieving it. Planning should be based on the assets available to an agency and a projection of resources needed to meet the goal. A good plan will show how differing entities interrelate and may reveal unexpected consequences. Planning brings resources together in a complex environment to manage multiple consequences. The complexities of terrorism can seem overwhelming, so planning is essential. (See Box 5.4.)

Planning is crucial for proactive counterterrorism. As Bodrero (2002) argues, gathering, organizing, and analyzing information is enhanced by planning. Police agencies have long been aware of the need to make reactionary plans. Emergency planning, for example, is a tool for weather disasters and industrial accidents. After the Metro Dade riots of 1980, local agencies developed field force deployment plans similar to mutual aid pacts among firefighters. The tragedies of Oklahoma City and September 11 brought several plans to fruition, and successful efforts in planning can be transferred into offensive strategies.

The International Association of Chiefs of Police (IACP, 2001) believes planning can be guided by looking for threats inside local communities. Police agencies should constantly monitor communities to determine whether a threat is imminent. Indicators such as an increase in violent rhetoric, the appearance

---

**BOX 5.5   Close-Up: Community Indicators
for Threat Assessment**

New activity in any of the following areas may indicate possible terrorist events. Watch for:

- Emergence of violent radical groups—squabbles among group members, especially religious organizations
- Appearance of violent radical literature
- Violent religions, cults, or groups
- New outside groups keeping to themselves
- Increase in hate crime or rhetoric
- Increase in international tension
- Suspicious subjects observing infrastructure facilities

- Individuals with connections to violent groups
- Growth of false charities
- Unexpected terrorist information found during search warrants
- Violent suspects using religious rhetoric and symbols during interviews
- Groups with links to foreign countries
- Appearance of clandestine bomb factories
- Illegal money used to fund political organizations

SOURCE: Institute for Intergovernmental Research.

---

of extremist groups, and increases in certain types of crimes may demonstrate that a terrorist problem is on the horizon. Planning is based on the status of potential violence, and law enforcement can develop certain responses based on the threat. Prepared responses, the IACP contends, are proactive. (See Box 5.5.)

Richard Best (12-3-01) points to another aspect of planning. National security differs from law enforcement, Best argues. In police work, officers react to information provided voluntarily. Police actions are governed by the rules of evidence, and the ultimate purpose is to protect the rights of citizens, including those who have been arrested. National security intelligence, on the other hand, is used to anticipate threats. It uses aggressive methods to collect information, including, at times, operations in violation of the law. National security intelligence is ultimately designed to protect targets, not individual rights. (See Box 5.6.)

Best quotes former Director of Central Intelligence (DCI) Stansfield Turner to summarize the differences between national security and law enforcement. Give the FBI a task, Turner once said, and it will attempt to complete the mission within the constraints of the law. Give the CIA the same mission, and it attempts to complete the task without concern for legality. This dilemma is indicative of a prime concern for law enforcement. It cannot abandon its public service role. Regardless of policy, the American police will lose public trust if they become the bulwark for covert operations. With Best's insight, law enforcement should plan and develop two channels for information.

One channel should be aimed at law enforcement intelligence; that is, the type of information police agencies collect. As Best (2001) describes, this information is based on criminal activity and the protection of individual rights. It is governed by the rules of evidence. Yet, police agencies will inevitably come

---

BOX 5.6   Close-Up: The Forms of Intelligence

Law Enforcement Intelligence— gathers information for criminal prosecution, criminal activities, criminal organizations, and to interdict criminal acts.

*Defense Intelligence—*gathers information to be used in national defense, enemy capabilities and organization, and probable military actions from America's enemies.

Force Protection Intelligence— gathers information about potential criminal and military actions against areas where American troops are deployed. It utilizes both law enforcement and defense intelligence, and it is similar to private industry's efforts to protect assets.

---

upon defense information, especially when monitoring community indicators. Much of this intelligence will not be used in criminal investigation. At this point, state and local police agencies should be prepared to pass such information along to defense sources. These two paths for information, one for criminal and one for national security, can serve as the basis for dealing with intelligence collected by state and local police agencies.

INFORMATION SHARING

The National Strategy for Homeland Security (2002, p. 56) calls for increased information sharing among law enforcement agencies. The reports say America will build a cooperative environment that enables sharing of essential information. It will be a "system of systems that can provide the right information to the right people at all times." This is an excellent idea in principle. (See Box 5.7.)

Bodrero (2002) points to systems already in place. The Regional Information Sharing System (RISS) is a six-part information network whose policies are controlled by its members. It is ideal for sharing intelligence. It has secure intranet, bulletin board, and conference capabilities. Bodrero points to two other regional databases, the High Intensity Drug Trafficking Areas (HIDTAs) system and the El Paso Intelligence Center (EPIC), as sources for information sharing. Another source is the International Association of Law Enforcement Intelligence Analysts (IALEIA). In addition, some states are looking to pool their resources in a common intelligence network.

Critics say these networks are underutilized. Robert Taylor (1987) finds two primary weaknesses in American systems: Intelligence is not properly analyzed and agencies do not coordinate information. Chad Nilson and Tod Burke (2002) claim law enforcement is the primary institution responsible for protecting America from terrorism by sharing information. Ironically, their finding is presented as a recommendation, not a description of current practices.

BOX 5.7 Close-Up: Homeland Defense Intelligence

The National Strategy for Homeland Security calls on all levels of government to

- Share information.
- Develop federal, state, and local law enforcement systems to share information.
- Develop common standards for electronic data.
- Improve public safety and public health communications.
- Establish five principles for information sharing:

- Balance security needs with individual freedoms.
- View federal, state, and local governments as one entity.
- Gather information by one source that will be distributed at many points.
- Create information databases on threats.
- Constantly update information.

SOURCE: Office of Homeland Security, 2002.

The Commission on National Security (2001), a group of fourteen nonpartisan former governmental officials, contends that rhetoric dominates discussions of intelligence sharing, but little sharing takes place in the real world. Although focused on police gang units, findings by criminologist Charles Katz (2001) offer a possible explanation for the failure to share information. Specialized units are formed as a result of a variety of political pressures. Police administrators are reluctant to trust them. If Katz is correct, the same logic will apply to high-profile homeland defense units.

Sociologist Peter K. Manning (1977) conducted one of the most definitive modern studies of policing. While on the surface it may appear dated, it contains a wealth of information about police attitudes and behaviors. In fact, it probably is the best single study of police customs and social actions ever written. Manning's work also explains the primary factor inhibiting cooperation not only among individual officers but also between agencies. The police have a problem with information, and there are rewards for keeping intelligence from other officers. The information gained by individual police officers creates organizational power. Officers who control large amounts of information increase their chances for success. Information is power, and there are few reasons to share it.

FBI Director Robert Mueller attended the International Association of Chiefs of Police Conference in Toronto in October 2001. In the words of one observer, he was "beaten up." American chiefs were upset with the FBI's unwillingness to share information. Moeller made a commitment, promising a new day of information sharing. Members of the Bush administration started calling for a "seamless interface" among systems (Office of Homeland Security, 2002, p. 43). Political rhetoric is easier to generate than changes in organizational culture. Secrecy is not the exclusive property of the FBI; it is culturally embedded in the smallest American police agency. Mueller is, however, correct. Information should be disseminated to the officers who need it. Despite the police obsession for secrecy, the reasons for not sharing intelligence crashed into the World Trade Center on September 11.

THE INEVITABLE FAILURE OF INTELLIGENCE

Despite the best intentions and the creation of better systems, intelligence will fail at certain points. Columbia University's Richard K. Betts (2002) explains why. He argues that reforms will be fast-tracked in the wake of September 11, and they will lead to more efficient systems and better skills among personnel. Yet, the awful truth is that intelligence will have major failures. Intelligence is competitive, and our enemies are trying to beat us. Terrorists only need to be successful one time.

Betts believes America should spend money on the systems that produce the biggest results for the smallest amount of money. The goal, he says, is not to spend money on new ideas and equipment, but to get the current system to increase its capabilities and performance. In Betts's words, America should do "more of everything and do it better." America can do this by collecting more critical information and relying less on machines and more on human intelligence agents and analysts.

Betts laments the real lack of linguistic and cultural diversity in organizations like the Central Intelligence Agency. We have few truly bilingual people and even fewer who are skilled in the culture and activities of remote parts of the world, he says. Preparing and hiring a variety of officers and analysts who are thoroughly trained in a variety of foreign cultures and who, when pooled together, provide a myriad of linguistic capabilities will enhance intelligence.

Yet, Betts says, even this will fail once in awhile. The best system cannot stop every attack. When prevention and interdiction can do no more, state and local law enforcement will be called to the scene to manage a crisis. In terms of homeland security, the mission will shift from offense to defense.

6

The Defensive Role
of Law Enforcement

Gathering and analyzing information are the most effective tools in counter-terrorism's offensive arsenal. Yet, intelligence and aggressive police actions will inevitably fail, and terrorists will eventually thwart the most aggressive law enforcement measures. In truth, the best offense will falter at times. Therefore, state and local law enforcement agencies need to prepare defensive plans; that is, they need to be prepared to react to terrorism. While a strategy solely based on defensive concepts leaves all the initiative with terrorist groups, ignoring the need to protect the public with defensive measures is irresponsible. In addition, even defensive actions can be offensive. For example, enhanced security may uncover a plan to attack a facility, or visible patrol presence may deter an attack. It is important to understand the symbolic nature of terrorist attacks and to balance security needs with basic freedom. State and local agencies should plan operations within the context of multi-jurisdictional responses and prepare a response for weapons of mass destruction. Understanding the importance of defending against and reacting to terrorist violence complements aggressive law enforcement actions.

After reading this chapter, you should be able to

1. Differentiate between a surprise military attack and terrorism.
2. Discuss the balance between security and openness as a symbol of democracy.
3. List and define the roles of various agencies involved in responding to a terrorist attack.

4. Outline the federal government's CONPLAN.

5. Summarize the problems posed by weapons of mass destruction.

6. List the issues involved in planning for a biological attack.

7. Define differing types of biological and chemical weapons.

8. Outline the defensive response to chemical and radioactive terrorism.

9. Summarize the importance of protecting critical infrastructures.

MILITARY SURPRISE ATTACKS AND TERRORISM

December 7, 1941 is known as "a day that will live in infamy"; September 11, 2001 is certainly a day that burned into the hearts of Americans. Both events held common surprises. For example, both Pearl Harbor and the suicide strikes indicated that America was vulnerable to attack. Both events occurred with no formal declaration of war and both involved civilian casualties. Pearl Harbor and September 11 also shook the soul of the United States.

Despite these similarities, September 11 differs significantly from Pearl Harbor. The purpose of the Japanese surprise attack was to destroy American military capabilities in the Pacific. Japanese governmental and military officials knew the United States would go to war as soon as the surviving Zeros returned to their carriers. The Japanese planned to destroy a military target to support attacks elsewhere, and they knew their action would result in war. By contrast, the September 11 hijackings were designed for drama. The purpose was to murder thousands of victims to create an aura of fear.

Nevertheless, the September 11 terrorists do not consider the actions murder (Lichtblau, 9–29–01). It their minds, strikes against symbolic targets are military actions, and civilian casualties hardly represent murder. Civilians associated with the enemy represent combatants (Juergensmeyer, 2000, pp. 143–155). The goal of the September 11 terrorists was not one of conventional military strategy. There was no grand offensive to follow the attacks and no notion of a rational, negotiated peace. The terrorists who targeted the United States wanted the West to believe that mass murder can happen at any time. They were sending the message that security measures, no matter how stringent, cannot protect citizens.

DEFENDING SYMBOLS AND STRUCTURES

Asymmetrical war is waged against symbolic targets; defensive strategies are designed to secure symbols. Just because a target has symbolic significance does not mean it lacks physical reality. The bombing of the Murrah Federal Build-

---

BOX 6.1   Close-Up: Protecting Communities and Symbols

Examine the following considerations for defensive planning. What other items might be added?

- Find networks in and among communities. Look at transportation, power grids and fuel storage, water supplies, industrial logistics and storage, and the flow of people.
- Think like a terrorist. Which targets are vulnerable? Which targets would cause the most disruption? Which buildings are vulnerable? Where is private security ineffective?
- Obtain plans for all major buildings. Protect air intakes, power supplies, and possible points for evacuation.
- Have detailed emergency information for each school. Practice tactical operations in each school building after hours.

- Prioritize. Assign a criticality rating to each target, assessing its importance, and rank targets according to comparative ratings.
- Coordinate with health services. Discuss triage and quarantine methods. Plan for biological, chemical, and radiological contamination.
- Don't reinvent the wheel. Look at emergency plans for other communities and utilize the appropriate methods.
- Prepare added security for special events.
- Designate an emergency command post and roles for personnel from other agencies. Practice commanding mock attacks.
- Study past emergencies and determine what law enforcement learned from its shortcomings.

---

ing in Oklahoma City in 1995, for example, had symbolic value, but the casualties were horrific. Attacks against symbols disrupt support structures and can have a high human toll. Defensive measures are put in place to protect both the physical safety of people and property as well as the symbolic meaning of a target (see Juergensmeyer, 2000, pp. 155–163 and Critical Incident Analysis Group, 2001, pp. 9–16). (See Box 6.1.)

Grenville Byford (2002) points out that symbolic targets may include civilian attacks. Killing civilians serves a political purpose for terrorists. American citizens contribute economically to the well-being of the country, and since they participate in a democracy, they ultimately control military policy. Targeting them, Byford argues, may have practical as well as symbolic value. Rather than engaging in political rhetoric about morality, Byford concludes, it is important to demonstrate that America will not accept defeat. Protecting symbols becomes one aspect of such a strategy.

Ian Lesser (Lesser et al., 1999, pp. 85–144) outlines three forms of terrorism: symbolic, pragmatic, and systematic. Symbolic terrorism is a dramatic attack to show vulnerability, and pragmatic terrorism involves a practical attempt to destroy political power. Systematic terrorism is waged over a period of time to change social conditions. Although identifying these three forms of terrorism, Lesser points to several examples where symbolic factors enter into attacks. In other words, terrorists use symbolic attacks or attacks on symbols to achieve pragmatic or systematic results.

The University of Virginia's Critical Incident Analysis Group (CIAG) brought a number of law enforcement officials, business leaders, government administrators, and academics together to discuss America's vulnerability to symbolic attack (CIAG, 2001). Symbols can have literal and abstract meanings, such as the case of a capitol that serves literally and abstractly as the seat of government power. The key to security is to offer protection without destroying abstract meanings. For example, the words of one CIAG participant summed up the problem: We want to protect the Capitol building, he said, without making Washington, D.C., look like an armed camp.

All societies create symbols and American democracy is not different. In a time of asymmetrical war, American symbols demand protection. The key to security, the CIAG concludes, is to enhance protection while maintaining openness, but every added security measure increases the feeling of insecurity. The CIAG report cites metal detectors at county courthouses. Simply going through the detector prior to entering gives the feeling that all things might fall apart. The irony of security is that it suggests some level of insecurity.

The Institute for Global Education (2001) notes this irony. The Institute assembled a panel of academics to discuss America's reaction to September 11, one of the topics involved enhanced security. Professor Burt DeVries discussed an encounter with security at a Michigan airport. As he stopped at a security gate, the security officer behaved officiously and rudely. DeVries sadly concluded that America was behaving more and more like a police state. The CIAG report warns against this. A democracy, the report concludes, must balance the need for security with general openness to all aspects of public life.

COORDINATING A MENAGERIE
OF AGENCIES

State and local police agencies will ultimately decide how deeply they become involved in homeland defense, but the nature of terrorism will force them to participate. When terrorists attack, local police officers are almost always the first government representatives to respond. Even if agencies choose not to develop aggressive counterterrorist intelligence systems, officers will still be called to terrorist scenes as "first responders." When the police arrive, they will interact with a host of other agencies.

American public service bureaucracies have developed several de facto roles and missions through historical evolution, and fire departments have inherited several responsibilities over the course of time. They have developed skills in responding to chemical spills, industrial disasters, and urban rescue. New threats brought increased training in nuclear and biological weapons in the 1990s. Firefighters are learning new roles as first responders to terrorism.

Other agencies complement law enforcement and fire department responses to homeland defense. They include the public health community, state-controlled military organizations, and private-sector security. Private companies and public agencies that provide basic services such as power, transportation, communication, information, and other infrastructure services may also have responsibilities. The federal government has recognized the crucial interface among these agencies, establishing the National Infrastructure Protection Center and ordering it in October 2001 to share information among the various entities. The Department of Homeland Security reiterated this call (Office of Homeland Security, 2002).

The defensive role for state and local law enforcement primarily involves responding to emergencies. As in the case of a large industrial accident or a natural disaster, various private and public agencies may assist with the police response. As in offensive operations, the key to reaction is planning. In a major disaster, state and local agencies will find themselves interacting with all levels of government and a variety of other agencies. Preparation for such events need not take place in a vacuum; experience with emergency response planning provides a guide. Furthermore, the federal government has provided extensive assistance with its own plans.

In early 2001 the federal government developed the Interagency Domestic Terrorism Concept of Operations Plan (CONPLAN), involving a system to coordinate the response of six federal agencies to domestic terrorism (CONPLAN, 2001). The agencies include the Department of Justice (DOJ), with the Federal Bureau of Investigation (FBI) as the lead agency; the Federal Emergency Management Agency (FEMA); the Department of Defense (DOD); the Department of Energy (DOE); the Environmental Protection Agency (EPA); and the Department of Health and Human Services (DHHS). By coordinating the response of its major agencies, the federal government hopes to interact effectively with state and local governments after a terrorist attack. The FBI is the lead agency during an attack, while FEMA assumes control afterward. (See Box 6.2.)

The federal government originally divided its defensive approach into two different operations, crisis management and consequence management. Crisis management refers to activities occurring while a terrorist incident is taking place. By federal definition, this is a law enforcement activity. While the federal government states that the supportive role of state and local law enforcement is crucial in crisis management, it gives the primary responsibility to federal agencies, specifically the FBI. The CONPLAN speaks about federal cooperation with state and local officers, but it can do nothing to establish a federal-state-local structure. This comes only when federal agencies join state and local agencies in planning, training, and intelligence sharing. Many jurisdictions have taken the initiative to integrate local plans into federal responses. For its part, the federal government sponsors joint exercises and evaluations. The New York City Police Department has even taken crisis management planning and training to a higher level, building a program in conjunction with the Naval War College (Baker, 4–25–02). (See Box 6.3.)

**BOX 6.2   Close-Up: Interagency Domestic Terrorism Concept
of Operations—The Law Enforcement Role**

The primary responsibility falls to the FBI. According to the CONPLAN:

> The Attorney General is responsible for ensuring the development and implementation of policies directed at preventing terrorist attacks domestically, and will undertake the criminal prosecution of these acts of terrorism that violate U.S. law. DOJ has charged the FBI with . . . the management of a Federal response to terrorist threats or incidents that take place within U.S. territory or those occurring in international waters that do not involve the flag vessel of a foreign country. As the lead agency for crisis management, the FBI will implement a Federal crisis management response. As LFA, the FBI will designate a Federal on-scene commander to ensure appropriate coordination of the overall United States Government response with Federal, State and local authorities until such time as the Attorney General transfers the overall LFA role to FEMA. The FBI, with appropriate approval, will form and coordinate the deployment of a Domestic Emergency Support Team (DEST) with other agencies, when appropriate, and seek appropriate Federal support based on the nature of the situation.

SOURCE: Quoted from CONPLAN, p. 3.

Consequence management refers to managing an event after an attack has occurred. FEMA is the lead agency in consequence management, and other federal, state, and local units of government are assigned supportive roles. By its own admission, the federal government has spent more resources in consequence management than in crisis management. State and local law enforcement have followed this trend. This organizational structure is time-tested, and the system has worked in both terrorist incidents and natural disasters. The only problem is that it can do nothing to prevent terrorism. Although effective, it is not a proactive policy.

Not everyone agrees with the idea of dichotomizing crisis and consequence management. A bipartisan committee on national security states that the federal government is spending too much time looking at the difference between crisis and consequence management (Commission on National Security, 2001). In addition, the committee argues that law enforcement will have the lead role in the initial stages of consequence management so time and effort are wasted by making false distinctions between the crisis and its consequences. Another commission (Cilluffo et al., 2001) advocates dividing the approach to terrorism into two categories, proactive and reactive, and it argues for integrating state and local law enforcement in each phase. The Bush administration recommends ending the dichotomy between crisis and consequence management (Office of Homeland Security, 2002).

**BOX 6.3   Close-Up: Federal Roles for Public
and Defense Agencies**

**The FBI Is the Lead Agency—Other
Federal Roles Include:**

*Federal Emergency Management
Agency (FEMA)*

- Coordinate consequence
management with state and local
governments
- Advise the FBI
- Assist with the deployment of the
Domestic Emergency Services Team
(DEST)
- Send representatives to operations
and information centers

FEMA's prime responsibility is for the
restoration of normality.

Department of Defense (DOD)

- Support the FBI
- Assist with crisis management
(assisting during an ongoing
incident)
- Provide technical assistance to law
enforcement
- Assist the FBI in tactical operations,
if requested
- Conduct threat assessments
- Provide transportation and
logistical support
- Transport and dispose of WMD
devices
- Restore order during civil
disturbances
- Respond to WMD incidents
- Provide the infrastructure for DEST
- Expand counterterrorist roles
when legally requested

DOD's prime responsibility is to
augment support and tactical
operations when situations threaten
national security and exceed the
abilities of other agencies to respond.

Department of Energy (DOE)

- Support FBI technical operations
- Support FEMA in consequence
management
- Provide scientific support during
WMD attacks

- Assist with threat assessments and
forecasting
- Provide technical support for
law enforcement tactical
operations
- Participate in WMD searches
- Provide diagnostic support with
suspected WMD
- Monitor effects of chemicals and
radiation

DOE's prime responsibility is to
provide scientific assistance during
chemical and radiological attacks.

*Environmental Protection
Agency (EPA)*

- Support FBI technical operations
- Support FEMA in consequence
management
- Coordinate with DOE during any
WMD attack
- Assist with threat assessments
- Monitor the environment after
any WMD attack
- Identify agents and other hazards
- Sample toxins and other
hazardous materials
- Supervise clean ups

EPA's prime responsibility is to contain,
control, and remove environmental
hazards after an attack.

*Department of Health and Human
Services (DHHS)*

- Support agency FBI technical
operations
- Assist FEMA with consequence
management
- Provide regulatory follow-up when
an incident involves a product
regulated by the Food and Drug
Administration.
- Support DEST deployments and
epidemiological investigations
- Assist with mass fatality
management
- Provide medical record services

(continued)

BOX 6.3   Continued

- May provide mass immunization,   DHHS's prime role is to assist with
  pharmaceutical support, and   public health management.
  patient evacuation

SOURCE: CONPLAN, 2001, pp. 4–6.

State and local law enforcement agencies may utilize federal preparations to assist in planning for responses to attacks. The IACP recommends incorporating existing responses in police emergency plans and rehearsing responses prior to an event (IACP, 2001). Ideally, local chiefs and sheriffs will prepare for a terrorist attack by operating in networks and planning to assist one another. The IACP urges police agencies to develop links with fire services, emergency medical facilities, public works, transportation, and federal agencies. It is not a question of either crisis or consequence management, it is necessary to do both, the IACP says, and rehearsing responses uncovers weaknesses. There is also an overlapping advantage in preparing for terrorism. If local departments have planned for a major terrorist event, many of the principles learned in multiagency counterterrorist rehearsals will be applicable to other disasters. (See Box 6.4.)

RESPONDING TO WEAPONS
OF MASS DESTRUCTION

One of the greatest threats of modern terrorism involves weapons of mass destruction (WMD). Ian Lesser (Lesser et al., 1999, pp. 85–144) believes religious fanaticism and the growth of nonstate terrorism help to provide an atmosphere conducive to the use of WMD. The IACP (2001) warns that WMD not only cause extensive casualties and damage to infrastructures, they can disrupt communities far from the site of an attack and psychologically devastate an entire country. In earlier times some of the best-known terrorism analysts did not think WMD were necessarily on the terrorist agenda (Jenkins, 1980, 1986, and 1987). The changing world of terrorism has caused many specialists to rethink the issue (Laqueur, 1999).

Preparation for WMD fall into several basic categories. Nuclear weapons include both atomic bombs and the dispersion of radioactive materials, so-called dirty bombs. Biological weapons involve bacterial microbes and viruses, and biological agents are said to be "weaponized" when a microbe is developed in a controllable, dispersible form. Chemical agents are dispersed as solids, liq-

---

BOX 6.4   Close-Up: The Department of Homeland Security Act 2002

President George W. Bush signed the Homeland Security Act into law on November 25, 2002. It has been touted to be the greatest reorganization of the federal government since the beginning of the Cold War. Several departments have been assigned to the new Secretary for Homeland Security. Some of the agencies transferred to the Department of Homeland Security (DHS) include the:

- United States Secret Service
- National Infrastructure Protection Center
- Energy Assurance Office
- National Communications System
- United States Coast Guard
- Customs Service
- Transportation Security Administration
- Federal Protective Service
- Functions of the Immigration and Naturalization Service
- Office of Domestic Preparedness
- Selected functions of the Department of Agriculture
- Federal Law Enforcement Training Center
- National Bio-Weapons Defense Analysis Center
- Nuclear threat assessment programs
- Federal Emergency Management Agency

- Domestic Emergency Support Team
- Metropolitan Medical Response System
- National Disaster Medical System
- Strategic National Stockpile of the Department of Public Health
- Nuclear Incident Response Team
- A new Bureau of Citizenship and Immigration Services

The new department is arranged under five Under Secretaries for:

- Information Analysis and Infrastructure
- Science and Technology
- Border and Transportation Security
- Emergency Preparedness and Response
- Management Services

The purpose of this massive reorganization is to centralize government planning and response. The DHS has been charged to cooperate and coordinate with state and local governments. The CIA and FBI remain separate agencies. How might the DHS affect relations among bureaucracies? Does it clarify the nebulous nature of low-level war? Will it enhance state and local planning? Does reorganization alone provide any incentive for state and local agencies to work more closely with the federal government?

---

uids, gases, or vapors. They do not last as long as biological agents, but they work more quickly and they are easier to control (IACP, 2001).

Michael Osterholm and John Schwartz (2000, pp. 189–191) argue that the United States has confused the law enforcement response to biological, chemical, and radiological attacks by lumping WMD into a single category. They are particularly upset by the label "chem-bio," which places biological and chemical attacks in the same category. They are two different types of attacks, Osterholm and Schwartz say, and they require different responses with appropriate types of specialists.

There are parallel skills for each of the WMD. These include evacuation, triage for mass casualties, containing the incident, and cleanup. All of these activities fall in the consequence management category as defined by the federal government. Yet, there are significant differences with the delivery of each weapon, which require specialized modes of response. One of the primary goals of state and local law enforcement should be to insist that all bureaucracies are prepared to respond to WMD and are willing to cooperate with other agencies. WMD represent a massive challenge to state and local infrastructures.

In addition, the role of law enforcement on every level changes in the event of a WMD attack. Law enforcement is not equipped to manage the results of WMD attacks, and it does not have the expertise to recognize the nature of the event. It is counterproductive to try to develop these skills in the law enforcement community because they are highly specialized—often requiring advanced degrees and research—and the knowledge for responding exists in other bureaucracies. Law enforcement has two critical roles in a WMD attack. The police should support agencies responding to a WMD attack and investigate the attack. Investigation will involve teamwork and cooperation among intelligence services and all levels of law enforcement. Responsibilities for assisting other agencies differ with each type of attack.

RESPONDING TO BIOLOGICAL THREATS

Biological weapons have been used for centuries. Modern arsenals contain bacterial and viral weapons with microbes cultured and refined (weaponized) to increase their lethality. When people are victimized by a bacterial attack, antibiotics may be an effective treatment. In the case of the September 2001 anthrax attacks in Florida, New York, and Washington, D.C., public health officials issued preventative antibiotics. Since bacterial agents are susceptible to antibiotics, nations with weapons programs have created strains of bacterial microbes resistant to medicines. Viral agents are produced in the same manner, and they are usually more virulent than bacterial agents and resistant to antibiotics. By the same token, some vaccines issued prior to the use of viral weapons prove to be effective (see Hinton, 1999 and Young and Collier, 2002).

The problem posed by biological weapons extends beyond the capabilities of all levels of law enforcement. Epidemiologists from the Center for Disease Control and Prevention (CDC) continually scan disease patterns in the United States to determine whether an outbreak is occurring, but there are serious weaknesses in the system. Osterholm and Schwartz emphatically argue that the public health system is not designed to handle massive casualties produced by a biological attack. The profit motive behind America's public health structure precludes planning for a worst-case scenario. Hospitals are designed to work at maximum cost effectiveness, and physicians are monitored by the amount of patient time they bill. Most physicians are not trained to recognize diseases such as anthrax, smallpox, and plague, and there is no economic incentive for them to gain necessary training. The public health structure does not provide economic incentives to produce hundreds of beds and trained medical personnel who can respond to an exotic biological disaster. Government reports agree (CSIS, 2001; and Office of Homeland Security, 2002, pp. 43–44).

There are four types of biological agents: natural poisons, viruses, various bacteria, and plagues (White, 2003c, p. 252). The CDC classifies the most threatening agents as smallpox, anthrax, plague, botulism, tularemia, and hemorrhagic fever. Michael Osterholm and John Schwartz (2000, pp. 14–23) summarize the effect of each. Smallpox is a deadly contagious virus. Past vaccinations are so old that they are no longer effective against the disease. Anthrax is a noncontagious bacterial infection, while plague can be transmitted from person to person. Botulism refers to food-borne illnesses, and weaponized tularemia would probably involve typhoid fever. Hemorrhagic fevers are caused by viruses. One of the most widely known hemorrhagic fevers is the Ebola virus. Bacterial agents can be treated with antibiotics, but the latter have limited or no effect on viral microbes.

America has experienced two notable biological attacks since 1980, and the weakness of the health system was exposed each time. Judith Miller, Stephen Engelberg, and William Broad (2001, pp. 13–33) outline the first modern use of biological terrorism in the United States. Engineered by Rajneeshees of the Bhagwan Shree cult near Antelope, Oregon, the attack occurred in September 1984. (Incidentally, the Miller et al. book *Germs* is one of the best nontechnical discussions of biological weapons on the market. It should be standard background reading in American police agencies.)

The attack occurred in two waves as Rajneeshee cultists sprayed food-poisoning bacteria on local salad bars. The attack resulted in hundreds of illnesses, and it serves as a warning to state and local law enforcement. The attack indicated that American police agencies are ill-prepared to deal with a biological incident, and the interface between law enforcement and public health fell apart in Oregon. It took a full year for authorities to realize that the outbreak of food poisoning—a wave overwhelming local hospitals—was the result of a deliberate action. Even though citizens suspected the Rajneeshees, police lacked the technical ability to investigate the crime, and health officials lacked the skills to conduct a criminal investigation. In short, the police could detect neither the microbes nor the patterns of illness necessary to prove a criminal case, while health officials could isolate the bacteria without locating its source. The Rajneeshee attack begs for a partnership between science and policing.

The second bioterrorism attack came in the wake of September 11. It began in Florida when two tabloid writers were infected by anthrax through the mail. One of the victims died. In the following days anthrax appeared again as NBC evening news received spores in the mail. Just as in the Rajneeshee attacks, there was an initial breakdown among corporate security, law enforcement, and public health personnel. Police and private security officers did not know how to respond, and local public health officials frequently did not know what to advise. The situation grew worse in October.

Senate Majority Leader Thomas Daschle's office received its regular mail delivery after lunch on Friday, October 12. Fortunately, staff members were in a class learning how to recognize suspicious packages that afternoon. When staffers returned to work on Monday, they opened Friday's mail. Someone noticed a white powdery substance in a letter. Alerted by information from Friday's class, the staffer took immediate action, perhaps saving many lives. The powder contained anthrax spores. By October 20, Congress continued to function, but it functioned from other locations.

According to reporter Laura Parker (1–23–02), Senator Daschle's office workers were exposed to the highest level of anthrax ever recorded. The dosage ranged from several hundred to three thousand times higher than the amount needed to kill a human being. On the day after the attack, nasal cultures indicated the infection was spreading rapidly, infecting 75 people, including a pizza delivery person who happened to be present when the letter was opened. Physicians at Bethesda Naval Hospital reserved a number of extra beds in preparation for more infections, but they differed on the way the attack should be treated. They settled on a 90-day regimen of antibiotics and administering vaccines. Some spores contaminated mail facilities, and two postal workers died after being infected in the government's mail distribution center in Brentwood. The Dirkson Office Building remained closed for three months and cost $14 million to clean up. (See Box 6.5.)

Osterholm and Schwartz (2000, pp. 19–20) say anthrax is a particularly effective killer. It is a natural bacterial toxin that has been enhanced by weapons programs. People can be infected by eating contaminated food (gastrointestinal anthrax), exposure through the skin (cutaneous anthrax), and by inhaling spores (inhalation anthrax). Inhalation is the most deadly form, but natural spores are so large that the body's natural defense provides quite a bit of protection. Miller, Engelberg, and Broad (2001, pp. 40–44) point to the history of bacterial weapons to show how the effectiveness of anthrax has been increased. Weaponized anthrax microbes are smaller than natural anthrax, and the outside shell is "hardened" so that it can exist in a variety of environments. When the microbes enter a friendly environment, such as the moist tissues of the respiratory system, spores open and begin to multiply. (See Box 6.6.)

It is not cost-effective to familiarize law enforcement personnel with diagnostic techniques, but they need to recognize dangers, understand procedures, and know general terms of biological terrorism. A Canadian study demonstrated that one-tenth of a gram of anthrax can infect a 10 by 18 foot room in ten minutes, entering the respiratory system with an amount 180 times greater than a lethal dose (Parker, 1–23–02, p. 6A). A suspected hot zone must be contained, and all people in the zone, including responders, need to be treated. The zone can remain contaminated for weeks unless properly decontaminated.

Rick Weiss, reporting in the *Washington Post* (10–18–01, p. A12), points to several terms police officers should know about anthrax and other biological weapons. *Weapons grade* means that the bacteria have been finely milled. *Virulence* refers to the microbe's ability to cause disease, and it is determined by the

---

BOX 6.5   Close-Up: The Anthrax Attacks—October to November 2001

The *Wall Street Journal* summarized the nation's deadly encounter with anthrax and focused on the difficulty of the police investigation. Reporters Mark Schoof and Gary Fields point to the following events:

- October 4—A photographer is infected in Florida and dies the next day.
- October 8—A second infection is discovered in the same newspaper office.

- October 12—NBC receives anthrax through the mail.
- October 15—U.S. Senate receives anthrax through the mail.
- October 18–23—Anthrax discovered in mail facilities.
- October 31—A hospital worker is infected and dies in New York City.
- November 21—An elderly woman in Connecticut is infected and dies.

SOURCE: Schoof and Fields, 3-25-02, *Wall Street Journal*, A20.

BOX 6.6   Close-Up: Responding to Biological Terrorism

Lead agencies

- Public health administrators, investigators, and responders
- Expand medical infrastructure units
- Link to political authorities
- Quarantine policy managers
- Vaccination and antidote system

Support agencies

- Law enforcement: transportation, curfew, and quarantine personnel
- Media relations

---

bacteria's genetic composition. Strains produced in American, Iraqi, and former Soviet labs are particularly virulent. The spores found in Florida, New York, and Washington were not. Virulence can be enhanced by genetic engineering, a process that transfers strands from one strain of the bacteria to another. *Resistance* refers to a microbe's ability to resist antibiotics. The Soviets engineered strains resistant to antibiotics. Three types of antibiotics work against nonresistant strains of anthrax: Ciprofloxacin (Cipro), penicillin, and tetracycline.

A report from the Center for Strategic and International Studies (CSIS) (Cilluffo et al., 2001, pp. 39–50) argues that biological terrorism is unique. Differing from other WMD scenarios, a biological terrorist attack will involve a period for the disease to incubate, time for it to spread, initial and secondary outbreaks, and efforts to control the spread. The CSIS believes public health agencies must be prepared to recognize and contain all the stages of a biological attack, and they must coordinate efforts with public service agencies. The final CSIS recommendation is to include the FBI in planning. The presence of federal law enforcement necessitates a role for state and local police agencies.

BOX 6.7   Close-Up: Basic Facts about Anthrax

Anthrax is an acute infectious disease caused by the spore-forming bacterium *Bacillus anthracis*.

- Anthrax most commonly occurs in hoofed mammals and can also infect humans.
- Symptoms of disease vary depending on how the disease was contracted, but usually occur within seven days after exposure.
- The serious forms of human anthrax are inhalation anthrax, cutaneous anthrax, and intestinal anthrax.
- Initial symptoms of inhalation anthrax infection may resemble a common cold. After several days, the symptoms may progress to severe breathing problems and shock.
- Inhalation anthrax is often fatal.
- The intestinal disease form of anthrax may follow the consumption of contaminated food and is characterized by an acute inflammation of the intestinal tract. Initial signs of nausea, loss of appetite, vomiting, and fever are followed by abdominal pain, vomiting of blood, and severe diarrhea.
- Direct person-to-person spread of anthrax is extremely unlikely, if it occurs at all. Therefore, there is no need to immunize or treat contacts of persons ill with anthrax.
- In persons exposed to anthrax, infection can be prevented with antibiotic treatment.
- Early antibiotic treatment of anthrax is essential—delay lessens chances for survival.
- Anthrax usually is susceptible to penicillin, doxycycline, and fluoroquinolones.
- An anthrax vaccine also can prevent infection. Vaccination against anthrax is not recommended for the general public to prevent disease and is not available.

SOURCE: Reproduced from "Basic Facts about Anthrax," Center for Disease Control and Prevention, September 2001.

The most important aspect of the law enforcement role in a biological attack is to support the public health system. Local chiefs and sheriffs should have regular contact with public health officials to ensure realistic responses from law enforcement. Quarantine policy, usually outdated in most jurisdictions, is of prime importance in the event of contagious disease. Planners must develop methods for quarantining large areas, enforcing the quarantine, and maintaining security. It is quite possible that officers will be separated from family members who have been exposed to a deadly agent. Law enforcement should also be prepared to assist with the rapid expansion of health facilities into public buildings and to maintain open routes to a quarantined area. Psychologically, officers should be trained to deal with massive casualties. Administratively, some officers will be physically infected and some will be psychologically unable to function. Mutual support pacts—so long a practice in fire services—and clear lines of authority should be established before the event. (See Box 6.7.)

BOX 6.8 Close-Up: Basic Facts about Smallpox

- Smallpox infection was eliminated from the world in 1977.
- Smallpox is caused by variola virus.
- The incubation period is about twelve days following exposure.
- Initial symptoms include high fever, fatigue, and head and back aches.
- A characteristic rash, most prominent on the face, arms, and legs, follows in two to three days.
- The rash starts with flat red lesions that evolve at the same rate. Lesions become pus-filled and begin to crust early in the second week. Scabs develop and then separate and fall off after about three to four weeks.
- Smallpox kills 30 percent of its victims.
- Smallpox is spread from one person to another.

- Persons with smallpox are most infectious during the first week of illness, because that is when the largest amount of virus is present in saliva. However, some risk of transmission lasts until all scabs have fallen off.
- Vaccination against smallpox is not recommended to prevent the disease in the general public.
- In people exposed to smallpox, the vaccine can lessen the severity of or even prevent illness if given within four days after exposure.
- There is no proven treatment for smallpox.
- Patients with smallpox can benefit from supportive therapy (intravenous fluids, medicine to control fever or pain, etc.) and antibiotics for any secondary bacterial infections that occur.

SOURCE: Reproduced from "Basic Facts about Smallpox," Center for Disease Control and Prevention, 2001.

It is best to plan for these events before they happen rather than to simply react. The CSIS (Cilluffo et al., 2001, p. 44) recommends that law enforcement be prepared to:

1. Compel providers to supply stockpiles of antibiotics and vaccines.
2. Be protected from liability for supporting and prioritizing treatment resources.
3. Have the authority to search for biological weapons.
4. Have access to intelligence data.
5. Be given full control of deceased persons.

Osterholm and Schwartz (2000, pp. 183–188) also suggest planning to integrate law enforcement powers with public health, and vaccinating teams of officers for work in hot zones. (See Box 6.8.)

RESPONDING TO CHEMICAL
AND RADIOLOGICAL THREATS

The massive power and heat from atomic bombs place nuclear weapons in a class of their own, but chemical and radiological attacks are basically similar. Radiological poisoning and "dirty" radioactive devices are forms of chemical alterations. Chemicals are usually easier to deliver than biological weapons, and they are fast-acting. Radiological devices are slower than most chemicals, but their poison lasts longer and they can be spread like chemicals. Radioactive materials are also more resistant to heat than chemicals, so bombs or other heat-producing devices can be used to scatter them.

There is a good-news-bad-news juxtaposition with respect to chemical and radiological attacks. On the good-news side, American firefighters have quite a bit of training and experience in responding to chemical and radiological incidents. In addition, they know how to contain areas, and they can manage chemical situations more easily than biological attacks. State and local systems have experience in the chemical arena, but not all the news is good. With the exception of large metropolitan areas and jurisdictions with chemical plants, local agencies may not be prepared for chemical and radiological attacks. The reason: training and equipment are expensive (Hinton, 1999 and U.S. General Accounting Office, 1999).

According to the CSIS (Cilluffo et al., 2001, p. 35), Congress attempted to remedy the situation by increasing uniformity in local jurisdictions. The Defense Against Weapons of Mass Destruction Act (popularly known as the Nunn-Lugar-Domenci Act) authorized and provided funding for standardized training in 157 American cities. The only problem with the idea is that several hundred other jurisdictions need to be included. Training and response require expensive equipment.

Apart from the CSIS recommendations, there are two other factors affecting the abilities of local jurisdictions. First, state and local Hazardous Materials (HazMat) teams have experience responding to industrial and transportation accidents involving the spread of deadly chemicals and radioactive waste. In addition, the Department of Defense has quite a bit of historical experience with chemical weapons (White, 2003, p. 251). These factors favor state and local law enforcement as police agencies will generally be used to support HazMat teams and fire departments in the immediate vicinity of a chemical or radiological attack.

Chemical agents come in four basic varieties: nerve agents, blood agents, choking agents, and blistering agents. Radiological weapons would produce short-term burns and long-term contamination and health problems. Nerve agents enter the body through ingestion, respiration, or contact. Blood and choking agents are usually absorbed through the respiratory system, and blistering agents burn the skin and internal tissue areas upon contact (Organization for the Prohibition of Chemical Weapons, 2000). Radiological poisoning takes place when a contaminated material comes in contact with any source

---

BOX 6.9   Close-Up: Chemical Agents and Their Effects

AGENT	COMMON ENTRY	EFFECT
Nerve	Food, water, air, skin contact	Convulsions, flood of body fluids
Blistering	Skin contact, air	Burns
Choking	Air	Respiratory failure
Blood	Breathing, skin contact	Failure of body functions
Radiological	Food, air, water, skin contact	Burns, long term illness

---

BOX 6.10   Close-Up: Chemical Terrorism

Lead agencies
- Fire department
- Medical First responders
- Triage medical personnel
- First aid
- Medical evacuation

Support agencies
- Law enforcement—Secure control zone
- Medical—treatment at expanded sites
- DOD—experience and military history

---

that conducts radiation. The new material, such as contaminated food, water or metal, becomes an object that could poison humans. Small contaminated pieces of matter can also become a means of spreading radiation through the air (U.S. Congress, Office of Technology Assessment, 1995). (See Box 6.9.)

Even though public bureaucracies have experience with chemical and radiological agents, state and local law enforcement agencies will optimize planning and operational capabilities when interacting with other departments (Office of Homeland Security, 2002, pp. 41–46 and 55–58). Police agencies will play a supporting role to fire and health responders in the immediate area of the attack. This means that plans for coordinated responses increase police effectiveness when they are planned, practiced, and revised (IACP, 2001). Law enforcement also needs clear policy guidelines for authority to react and control activities inside and around the scene. The first responsibility is to help fire and medical personnel and evacuate victims. The legal aspects of control must be worked out prior to the attack. The CSIS (Cilluffo et al., 2001, pp. 37–39) recommends realistic training and coordination of state and local efforts. (See Box 6.10.)

As with biological terrorism, state and local officers must be trained to recognize the characteristics of chemical and radiological attacks (see Osterholm and Schwartz, 2000 and CSIS). Even in their supporting roles, the police will

---

BOX 6.11   Close-Up: Responding to Radiological Terrorism

Lead agencies
- Fire department
- Radiological response teams
- Nuclear Emergency Search Teams
- Control, triage, evacuation personnel

Support agencies
- Law enforcement—secure and stabilize
- Enact disaster plan
- Medical treatment at expanded sites
- DOD—utilize experience

---

be expected to collect and preserve evidence, and psychologically, local and state officers should be trained to deal with mass casualties. Aggressive investigations may prevent other actions. Finally, state and local police must be prepared to enforce martial law. (See Box 6.11.)

Before moving to the next section, it is also necessary to briefly mention nuclear terrorism. A stolen nuclear bomb or an atomic blast conjure the worst images of mass destruction. If nuclear terrorism happens, federal authorities will most likely respond with military support. The United States has plans and expertise in nuclear disasters, and the DOD has the monopoly on knowledge. The specter of nuclear terrorism requires old Cold War issues to be resurrected. Law enforcement will play a supporting role, and plans and command structures need to be in place before the event. Response plans will mirror those of a horrid natural disaster.

LAW ENFORCEMENT
AND THE INFRASTRUCTURE

A final defensive role for local law enforcement deals with the identification and protection of critical infrastructures. Information, energy, communication, transportation, and economic systems are vulnerable to terrorist attack. Their vulnerability requires law enforcement to develop new capabilities to provide protection. The Department of Homeland Security (Office of Homeland Security, 2002, pp. xi–xii) states that law enforcement agencies will need to develop cooperative links with all agencies involved in defensive measures, including private security. Fortunately, state and local police agencies are not starting in a vacuum. Both governmental agencies and private industry have recognized the need to provide security. In addition, many local chiefs and sheriffs have close relations with business and industry within their jurisdictions.

The Department of Homeland Security applauds efforts to coordinate resources, but critics feel too little is being done. Jeanne Cummings (8–13–02) points to two primary weaknesses. Even a year after September 11, the federal

---

BOX 6.12   Close-Up: Planning Infrastructure Protection

President William Clinton issued a directive declaring law enforcement to be part of the nation's critical infrastructure. Shortly after taking office, the Bush administration published a report based on the directive. It says:

- Each law enforcement agency is responsible for the protection of its own infrastructure. The United States government mandates federal agencies to develop plans and encourages local agencies to do so.
- Local plans should be flexible, based on the recommended

model but applicable to individual needs.

- Because police agencies use information systems, each department is asked to review its infrastructure and assess vulnerabilities. Factors recommended for the threat assessment include evaluating critical missions and capabilities, critical assets, critical interdependent relations, types of threats, and vulnerability to attack.
- Planning for protection should be based on a prioritized listing of critical services and vulnerabilities.

SOURCE: Emergency Law Enforcement Service Sector, 2001.

---

government had failed to release resources to state and local governments. State emergency planners complain they received little federal direction and no federal money. Cummings says the problem is even worse in the private security industry. Conducting a survey of America's largest shopping mall in Minnesota, Cummings concludes that federal law enforcement does little to assist private security. Keeping Americans safe, Cummings says, depends on state and local efforts outside Washington.

Richard Clarke, a Special Advisor to the President with an impressive bipartisan service record, testified before the Senate Subcommittee on the Judiciary on February 13, 2002. He outlined many of the threats facing the nation's infrastructure, painting a grim picture. Most computer systems are vulnerable to viruses, Clarke believes, because customers will not pay for proper protection. The government has opened more communication channels with users and vendors, but more protection is needed. Clarke says the power system and technological organizations are vulnerable to disruptions in Internet grid systems. Pointing to the railroad industry, Clarke shows how many "low tech" organizations have imported "high tech" support systems. Shut down electrical grids and computers, Clarke maintains, and you'll shut down transportation and communication. (See Box 6.12.)

As Clarke stated in testimony, the FBI should not have been the lead agency for infrastructure protection; the role is more suited to technological specialists. (On November 25, 2002, the Bush administration ordered the National Infrastructure Protection Center to move to the Department of Homeland Security.) Extending Clarke's logic, it can also be argued that state

---

BOX 6.13   Close-Up: Planning to Prevent Cyber Attacks

The Institute for Security Technology Studies at Dartmouth College recommends following the "best practices" of security in the computer industry. Best practices include:

- Update software.
- Enforce rigid password security.

- Disable unnecessary services.
- Scan for viruses and use virus protection.
- Utilize intrusion detection systems.
- Maintain firewalls.

SOURCE: Michael A. Vatis, 2001, p. 19.

---

and local law enforcement should not play the leading role in infrastructure protection. The key is to develop relationships so state and local police agencies can support security functions. (See Box 6.13.)

Protection of the infrastructure comes not with technical expertise equivalent to that of industrial specialists; it comes when specialists in crime fighting and protection establish critical links with organizations serving as America's infrastructure. Linkages should be developed in two crucial areas. First, the police should be linked to the security forces already associated with infrastructure functions. The American Society of Industrial Security (ASIS International) has made great strides in this area and more needs to be accomplished. State and local law enforcement agencies must establish formal and informal networks with the organizations in their jurisdictions, and these networks should expand to a cooperative federal system.

Michael Vatis (1999) points to another area. Police agencies need to become involved in the protection of their own information infrastructures. Following the trend in most American organizations, police agencies integrate electronic management and records systems in everyday routines. If these systems are disrupted, police agencies could lose their ability to function. Surveying major agencies throughout the country, Vatis argues that infrastructure defense begins at home.

7

Terrorism and the Future of Law Enforcement

American law enforcement has been charged with safeguarding lives and property throughout its history. At times, such as during an anarchist bombing campaign of 1919, it has faced emergencies that would be called terrorism today. At other times, like the repression of steel and coal unions in Pennsylvania in the late 1800s and early 1900s, it repressed a certain class of people to benefit another. How will it respond to the current threat of international terrorism? Will violent domestic extremists be confronted in the same manner as international terrorists? Will the police play a more military role if they become involved in national defense? Can state and local law enforcement develop a role in national defense and still maintain their crime-fighting and social service activities? Will the civil liberties of Americans be protected? Answers to these questions will develop as homeland security evolves on a national level. If we want to develop the best responses for democracy, it is important to consider the implications for the future.

After reading this chapter, you should be able to

1. Explain possible future sleeper cell tactics based on al Qaeda's training manual.

2. Discuss two positions regarding the militarization of police agencies.

3. List and define the types of domestic extremists facing law enforcement.

4. Cite the nations most frequently targeted by terrorism.

5. Explain why terrorists frequently target the United States.

6. Summarize probable future trends in terrorism.

AL QAEDA SLEEPER CELLS

The two founders and leaders of al Qaeda, Osama bin Laden and Aymaan al Zawahiri, subscribe to the puritanical doctrines of a violent religious strain and that movement will continue despite the fate of al Qaeda's leadership. Holy warriors still require tactics, logistics, training, and leadership. They may be motivated by religion, but sacred rage is no substitute for a good plan. Al Qaeda based terrorist attacks on a three-tiered model. Its most effective operations were carried out by cells attacking in conjunction with the group's leadership in Afghanistan. However, it also utilized two other methods, sleeper cells attacking on their own apart from centralized command and individuals supported by small cells. In late 2001 the United States launched a devastating offensive against al Qaeda, destroying its central command. The offensive dispersed survivors throughout the world (Nordland et al., 8–19–02, pp. 34–41).

The second and third tiers of al Qaeda are alive and well, surviving on every continent except Antarctica. American law enforcement and national intelligence agencies will encounter sleeper cells over the next few years. The terrorist cells do not represent mainstream Islam, but the violent strain of the puritanical Unitarian movement is so strong that new organizations will appear as al Qaeda cells are eliminated. The role of state and local agencies will evolve during the course of this struggle. The police can become effective partners in homeland defense if they understand how these cells operate. Box 7.1 provides a summary of al Qaeda operational guides.

MILITARIZATION AND POLICE WORK

Throughout much of this book you were asked to consider various aspects of the law enforcement role in national security, even including segments on theories of war. There are roles state and local police may play inside a system of homeland defense, but there are questions about the necessity of developing these functions on military lines. Some policymakers have responded by increasing the military posturing of the police. In other words, some police agencies have developed units that appear more suited for military functions than police work. On the other hand, some administrators and critics stress the civilian aspect of law enforcement, and they lament the paramilitary approach to controlling social problems. The debate between these two approaches will become more intense as the police role in homeland defense is institutionalized over time.

Before discussing the issue, let's define "militarization." Military forces are necessary for national defense, and they are organized along principles of rigid role structures, hierarchies, and discipline. A military posture prescribes

BOX 7.1 Close-Up: The Al Qaeda Manual

Law enforcement agencies have seized several copies of the al Qaeda manual, both from raids prior to September 11 and after allied military forces occupied terrorist training camps in Afghanistan. Differing versions of the manual offer variations. This CLOSE-UP contains a summary of the most important points in a version seized by the Manchester Constabulary in the United Kingdom. To review the manual in full, see *www.fbi.gov.*

The al Qaeda Manual begins by referencing several Islamic themes and justifying terrorism in the name of Islam. Several verses of the Koran are interspersed in the call to holy war (*jihad*).

First Lesson
A general introduction begins with a lamentation on the state of a the world, concluding with another call to holy war. The practical aspects of this section include an outline of the principles of military organization, requirements for terrorist operations, and a general strategy, including a list of potential targets.

Second Lesson
This segment focuses on the qualities of individual al Qaeda members. An organizational member must be a Muslim. The manual asks, "How can an unbeliever, someone from a revealed religion [Christian, Jew], a secular person, a communist, etc., protect Islam and Muslims and defend their goals and secrets when he does not believe in that religion [Islam]?" The section goes on to require several characteristics for membership, including commitment to the cause, maturity, willingness to sacrifice and obey orders, ability to keep secrets, and other military characteristics. It reinforces these qualities with references to the military history of German spies in World War I and in ancient Rome. It quickly shifts to practical discussions of intelligence-gathering activities in modern times.

Third Lesson
The third lesson focuses on forgery. It gives instructions on monetary security, forging identification papers, and maintaining security during an operation. While al Qaeda members have been captured with multiple false documents, the manual instructs them to use only one identity at a time.

Fourth Lesson
Focusing on safe houses and other hiding places, this segment provides instructions for establishing a clandestine terrorist network. It gives in-depth instructions for security surrounding the apartment of sleeper cells, teaching al Qaeda members to blend into their surroundings.

Fifth Lesson
This lesson is about secret transportation and communication. Contacts are to be quick and to the point, and only commanders are authorized to initiate communication. Members are told to use public phones on main streets, employing booths where possible. Conversation should be encoded, telephones should be switched periodically, and members are told to distort their voices. When al Qaeda members suspect a phone has been tapped, they are to provide false information on a long-term basis. This section also contains a lengthy discussion of security during face-to-face meetings and the use of messengers and letters.

The fifth lesson gives instructions in the use of public and private transportation. Regarding public conveyance, terrorists are taught to use busy carriers not subject to continual security checks. Boarding takes place at secondary terminals with light security, while switching occurs in larger airports, or train or

(continued)

BOX 7.1   Continued

bus stations. Members should mirror their social surroundings and fit the general appearance of travelers. Nondescript luggage should be placed with general passenger bags and contain no identification. If the luggage is seized by security, the member is to abandon it. Conversation should not be initiated with cab drivers or others. In private transportation, the manual urges members to obey traffic laws and to be nondescript. Vehicles owned by al Qaeda are not to be used in terrorist operations.

Sixth Lesson
This section discusses training and security during training. It is interesting to note that al Qaeda members construct a local infrastructure and train inside the geographical area where they attack. This segment also explains the dual approach to most al Qaeda operations. A local group operates inside the country to be attacked, using local materials and resources to support the attack, while a command group from outside the country provides operational control and additional logistics. Historically, this training and managerial style has been effective. (This is the first style of al Qaeda operations.) Sometimes, however, individual cells act on their own or individual terrorists go on a lone mission. (These are the cells presenting a problem to law enforcement.)

Seventh Lesson
Weapons, one of the keys to terrorism, are covered here. The manual gives instructions on obtaining weapons and transporting them. It also contains information on building an arsenal and safely storing explosives.

Eighth Lesson
The eighth lesson discusses secrecy and member safety. It stresses secrecy inside a cell and measures to hide true identities. One of the points stressed in this section emphasizes the need to maintain family and neighborhood ties in the operational area. Every instruction stresses the need to blend in and not to attract attention.

Ninth Lesson
A lengthy discussion of security, this section emphasizes planning and operations. It walks the would-be terrorists through target selection, planning, travel, attacking, and returning. You should note how terrorists differ from other criminals. If typical criminals do not plan operations, terrorists represent the antithesis. This section demonstrates not only extensive planning by al Qaeda members, but it teaches terrorists how to plan. Secrecy is stressed time and again.

Tenth and Eleventh Lessons
Lessons ten and eleven focus on reconnaissance. After providing a theological justification for dishonest behavior, this section teaches members how to use open sources from the media. It also contains methods for clandestine spying, including capturing prisoners. The manual tells members when to torture hostages and when to kill them, providing theological rhetoric along the way.

Twelfth Lesson
    This section continues the discussion of intelligence gathering, but it specifically focuses on covert methods. It also provides information on counterintelligence, that is, tactics intelligence gatherers use to ensure no one is gathering information

BOX 7.1 Continued

about their own operations. Al Qaeda operatives are taught such tactics as

1. Walking down dead-end streets to see who is following.
2. Dropping something to see who might pick it up.
3. Suddenly stopping and watching who is affected.
4. Standing in front of windows to observe reflections.
5. Getting on a bus and getting off before it starts.

The twelfth lesson instructs members to gain information about government workers, including their lifestyles, spouses and children, routines, and schedules. It also asks members to gather information about specific targets. Operatives are told to gain intelligence about

1. Buildings
2. Military bases
3. Government and business facilities
4. Airports
5. Seaports
6. Border crossings
7. Embassies
8. Radio and TV stations

After a lengthy set of instructions on surveillance, members are told to sketch the area after making a general photograph. The manual also gives instructions on recruiting informants, interviewing, and interrogating kidnapped hostages. This section concludes with discussions on profiles of American intelligence agents and methods for recruiting anti-American agents.

Intermediate Sections
A practical segment between lessons twelve and eighteen gives tips on handling recruited agents and dealing with counter measures. Al Qaeda operatives are taught to watch for booby traps and when to assassinate potential enemies. This intermediate section also teaches terrorists how to train other terrorists.

Eighteenth Lesson
The final section of the manual captured by the Manchester Constabulary contains instructions concerning behavior when arrested. Al Qaeda seems to have a working knowledge of the rights of prisoners in Western justice systems, and members are instructed to use individual rights for the benefit of the organization.

unquestioning obedience to orders and aggressive action in the face of an enemy. As you learned earlier, in Clausewitz's sense, military forces are either at war or at peace, and when engaged in war, their efforts are targeted toward an enemy. Any bureaucracy can be militarized when it adopts military postures and attitudes, and the police are no exception. If the United States is engaged in a "war" against terrorism, some policymakers will inevitably want the police to look more and more like a military force, especially because the Constitution prevents the American armed forces from enforcing domestic law. In this context militarization refers to a process where individual police units or entire agencies begin to approach specific problems with military values and attitudes. They adopt paramilitary dress, behave with military discipline, and, most importantly, they prepare to make war with an enemy.

In 1967 the International Association of Chiefs of Police (IACP) discussed the problem of confronting violent demonstrators (IACP, 1967, pp. 307–327). The late 1960s was a time of social change and violent confrontation, and state and local police frequently found themselves facing large hostile crowds. In response, the police often imported military maneuvers to control violent demonstrations and the tactics were successful. The IACP, however, was not quick to jump on a military bandwagon. The training manual instructs police officers to employ minimal criminal authority to solve potential problems. The appearance of paramilitary force was a last resort, and it developed only when the situation had deteriorated. The IACP, America's largest association of state and local police executives, has traditionally favored the civil role of policing over a militaristic approach.

Terrorism may bring a change in attitudes. For example, since many forms of terrorism require resources beyond the capacity of local police agencies, law enforcement has been forced to turn to the military for assistance. State and local law enforcement have few international resources when compared to the defense and intelligence communities. Finally, terrorism demands a team approach. Law enforcement officers exercise quite a bit of individual discretion when operating on calls or initiating activities, and they generally work alone or in small groups of twos and threes. Terrorism, like special events, changes the equation, bringing hundreds of officers together in a single function. The temptation may be to militarize the police response to terrorism.

Two trends may be seen in this area. The first comes from violent demonstrations. The Metro-Dade Police Department developed a technique for responding to urban riots after a particularly bad riot in 1980. It was called the "Field Force" technique and it was effective. By 1995 hundreds of American police agencies utilized the process, and it seems firmly established in the early years of the twenty-first century. The concept is based on responding to a growing disorderly crowd, a crowd that can become a precursor to a riot, with a massive show of organized police force. Officers assemble in an area away from the violent gathering, isolate the area providing a route for the crowd to disperse, then overwhelm it with military riot tactics. When watching a field force exercise, it looks as though a small army has moved into an area utilizing nonlethal violence (see Christopher, 1999, pp. 398–407 and Kraska and Kappeler, 1999, pp. 435–449).

A second source of militarization comes from police tactical units. These special operations units are called out to deal with barricaded gunmen, hostage situations, and some forms of terrorism. They are also frequently used on high-risk drug raids. Tactical units use military weapons, small unit tactics, and recognized military small unit command structures (see Cappel, 1979; Jacobs, 1983; and Mattoon, 1987). In the past few years many of the units have abandoned the blue or brown tactical uniforms of police agencies for military camouflage. When looking at such units, it is virtually impossible to distinguish them from military combat units.

Peter Kraska (1996) takes exception to these trends in militarization. He argues that the American police have gradually assumed a more military posture since violent standoffs with domestic extremists, and he fears terrorism will lead to a further excuse to militarize. This will adversely impact democracy, Kraska argues, because it will lead police to picture their jurisdictions as war zones and their mission as military victory. If the problem of terrorism is militarized, other social problems will follow. Kraska's point is well taken. As Michael Howard (2002) states, calling our struggle with terrorism a "war" creates a variety of conceptual problems. In addition, Americans have become used to military metaphors for other social problems such as "wars" on drugs or poverty.

Most terrorist analysts believe terrorism is best left to the police whenever possible (see Wardlaw, 1982, pp. 87–102). The difficulty is that the growing devastation of single events sometimes takes the problem beyond local police control. In addition, (DOD, 1–9–01 and Perl, 2001) military forces are often targeted, and they must develop forces to protect themselves. Some of the same principles guiding military force protection will eventually spill into American policing. As the future develops, state and local police may often find themselves in the midst of subtle social pressure to militarize the terrorist problem and respond to it with paramilitary force.

DOMESTIC EXTREMISTS STILL REMAIN

While much of the country is focused on international terrorism, you should not forget America's violent domestic extremists. They also cause problems. In fact, based on research since September 11 (Dyson, 2002), in the first six months after the World Trade Center attacks, domestic extremists accounted for far more destruction than international terrorists. (See Box 7.2.)

The FBI (2001) categorizes three types of domestic terrorism. Single-issue extremists are a growing problem in America, destroying more property in the name of animal rights, genetic engineering, and the environment than any other domestic group. Some antiabortion extremists have resorted to bombings and murder. Political terrorism refers to left- and right-wing violent extremism, racially motivated violent groups, and violent eschatological organizations. The final category identified by the FBI are lone criminals conducting their own campaign. "Berserkers" leave normative society and wage war within a personal construction of reality.

There are other classification systems. Paul Wilkinson (1974, 1986, and 1994), one of the "deans" of counterterrorist analysts, dichotomizes terrorism between political and criminal activities. H. H. A. Cooper (1976), another one of counterterrorism's founding scholars, predated many experts by offering a system designed by a presidential panel. Prior to the current federal typology, the FBI utilized another classification system based on the orientation of violent groups (Harris, 1987). I developed a five-fold typology of domestic terrorism based on

---

BOX 7.2   Close-Up: Right-Wing Calls for Revolution

Al Qaeda received much attention after September 11, but other terrorist threats remain. William Pierce, who led the extremist National Alliance from Hillsboro, West Virginia, called for white people to establish a racially pure culture. Such opinions stood behind another attack in the United States, the bombing of the federal building in Oklahoma City on April 19, 1995. Examine some of the following ideas espoused by Pierce in two right-wing fantasy novels, *Hunter* and *The Turner Diaries:*

- Utilizing fertilizer bombs to destroy federal facilities
- Infiltrating police agencies
- Storing illegal firearms and bombing equipment
- Individual murders of political opponents and non-whites
- Using a suicide airplane attack to destroy the Pentagon
- Lone sniper attacks against citizens engaged in everyday routines
- Mass execution of race traitors and intellectuals
- Obtaining WMD from military bases

---

political and criminal orientation in an IACP publication a few years ago. You could develop a typology as valid or with more accuracy than some classification schemes.

The point is not the manner of classification; the major issue is the police response to domestic terrorism. While international terrorism has fostered murky combinations of law enforcement and military activity, the response to domestic terrorism is ensconced in American criminal law, and as Dyson's research indicates domestic terrorism is far more prevalent than international terrorism. The state and local response to international terrorism will undoubtedly impact policies and procedures in the domestic arena. This work focuses on international terrorism, but it should be noted that the response to domestic terrorism may require the greatest amount of protection for civil liberties. International terrorism falls within the realm of a shadow war. Domestic terrorism involves criminal law.

FUTURE TRENDS
IN INTERNATIONAL TERRORISM

Bruce Hoffman (1998) and the staff from RAND (Lesser et al., 1999) summarize several interesting trends in modern terrorism, trends necessary to suggest future probabilities. D. Douglas Bodrero (2002) of the Institute for Intergovernmental Research also provides insight on the changing nature of international criminal extremists and their impact on American law enforcement. At the same time, Middle Eastern scholars have discussed the future of militant Islam (Esposito, 1999 and Kepel, 2002). A brief analysis of these findings will

---

**BOX 7.3   Close-Up: Trends Indicating Probable Actions
             in International Terrorism**

- The United States is the most frequently targeted nation.
- Terrorism is increasingly lethal.
- Incidents are declining, but results are more dramatic.
- Terrorism is increasingly based on religion.
- Terrorists make adaptations to changing technology.
- Terrorist structures are changing.

- Technological infrastructures will increasingly be targeted.
- International terrorists represent a new type of threat to law enforcement.
- Political Islam will continue to grow, but this does not necessarily mean it will clash with the United States.

SOURCES: Hoffman 1998 and 1999; Lesser et al., 1999; Bodrero, 2002; Esposito, 1999; and Kepel, 2002.

---

help project future trends in terrorism and the international problems facing state and local law enforcement. (See Box 7.3.)

Prior to 1983, international terrorism seemed to be an abstract problem for the United States. It was exotic, and when Americans were victimized, it could be most frequently associated with guerrilla war. The situation changed after Hezbollah bombed the U.S. Marine barracks in Lebanon. Bruce Hoffman (1999, pp. 35–36) explains that terrorists have now targeted the United States more than any other country. He believes this is due to America's diverse interests overseas and the availability of military and business targets. Terrorists are drawn to American targets because they symbolize everything wrong with the West. The news media acts as a force multiplier, giving an attack on any American target an added aura. In an asymmetrical setting, the United States often finds itself unable to respond effectively to terrorist attacks. Hoffman believes these factors will continue to make the United States an attractive target for terrorists. (See Box 7.4.)

Hoffman (1999, pp. 7–38) sees other interesting trends. The total number of international terrorist events is declining, but events are becoming more dramatic. Accompanying this dramaturgical surge is a trend toward increased lethality. In other words, terrorists are becoming more deadly. The lethal nature of terrorism has increased because terrorists have been able to adapt to technological changes in weaponry and defense measures. Changing structures in terrorist groups result in looser organizations where centralized authority figures put fewer constraints on terrorist operations. Groups are deadlier as a result. In earlier works, Hoffman (1995 and 1998, pp. 87–129) cites the rise of violent, intolerant religious extremism as another factor behind the increasing deadliness of terrorism. Since international terrorism has arrived on America's shores, state and local police will be called upon to deal with these factors.

John Arquilla, David Ronfeldt, and Michele Zanini (1999, pp. 39–84) believe technological infrastructures will increasingly fall prey to attack. They

---

BOX 7.4   Close-Up: The Top National Targets of International Terrorism

- United States
- Israel
- France
- United Kingdom
- Germany

- Russia
- Turkey
- Cuba
- Spain
- Iran

SOURCE: Hoffman (1999, p. 35).

---

base this prediction on three trends: Terrorist organizations are evolving into autonomous groups with technological abilities, their doctrines involve social disruption as well as destruction, and the groups are gaining the tools necessary to launch technological attacks. Terrorists use direct military-style electronic attacks on information systems and increasingly employ the Internet to disrupt logistics and communications. Future terrorists will improve their abilities to launch technological attacks.

Research by Michael Vatis (2001), analyzing computer attacks, agrees with the RAND projections. The most frequent tactic to date is to try to disrupt governmental and business communications on the World Wide Web. Future attacks, Vatis predicts, will reflect the cyberwar tactics defined by Arquilla and his fellow researchers. If state and local police choose to fully engage in homeland security, they will need to develop defensive links with electronic information experts.

D. Douglas Bodrero (2002) uncovers another disturbing trend. In the past, Bodrero argues, state and local law enforcement officers have been faced with untrained opportunists, criminals who differed from violent political extremists. This changed in the 1990s as officers found they increasingly met hardcore true believers, totally dedicated to an extremist cause. The international attack of September 11 reveals a new twist in terrorism. Officers are now being asked to face an enemy who uses criminal means to obtain a military objective. Terrorists are trained as soldiers, but they fight by violating criminal law. The new enemy expects to encounter American law enforcement; indeed, it has been trained to do so. The American police, Bodrero concludes, have not faced an enemy like this before. The extent to which state and local police will participate in homeland defense remains to be defined, but, as Bodrero points out, the enemy is not waiting for Americans to resolve the debate. It is prepared to attack American police officers on the home territory. The number of police casualties on September 11—the largest number of police officers to die in a single incident in American history—demonstrates the enemy's willingness to launch its attacks.

Finally, we cannot simply assume political Islam will disappear. It arose as a reaction to the ineffectiveness of postcolonial nationalism in Islamic counties. New rulers in Egypt, Turkey, Algeria, and other countries promised a better future through nationalism. Other nations, such as Iraq, embraced socialism under a national banner. These positions faltered, giving rise to political Islam.

John Esposito (1999, pp. 207–211) sees the sweep of political Islam across North Africa and the Middle East when Islamicist governments respond to local needs. The failure of postcolonial nationalism and socialism left a vacuum, Esposito argues, that is being filled by political Islam. Religious organizations are emerging throughout Africa and the Middle East, and many would be in power today if repressive governments did not keep them from power. He points to Tunisia, Algeria, Egypt, and Turkey as examples. Esposito believes that political Islam is firmly rooted in the near future.

Professor Gilles Kepel (2002) examines the same evidence, but his findings differ slightly from Espositos'. He feels that political Islam has run its course. Just as nationalist and socialist governments failed many Islamic nations after World War II, he argues that political Islam has failed to produce expected results. The reason, Kepel believes, is Islamic governments failed to deliver goods and services to the lower classes. They enlisted the poor in a broad coalition of middle-class professionals and clergy, but after coming to power, the poor remained poor. Islamicist governments have had their day. Former CIA director James Woolsey (7–29–02) agrees, at least with respect to Iran. The Islamic revolution of 1978–1979 failed to address the needs of the Iranian people, and Woolsey sees a new revolution where the mantle of the clergy will be overthrown.

Esposito and Kepel really offer variations on a theme. Whether Islamic governments rise or continue in power, political Islam will remain a factor in the near future, and it will be stronger in the areas where it responds to real needs. This is not necessarily bad for the United States. Both authors argue that America must constructively engage political Islam. As the United Kingdom's Prince Charles once said, the West has much more in common with Islam than it has differences. Regardless, violent extremists will remain and they will continue to target American interests.

Political Islam impacts American policing in three direct ways. First, Islamic culture is rich and diverse. As officers engage Muslim communities, they need not expect a clash of civilizations. Most Muslims came to the United States because they wanted to become Americans and enjoy American freedom. Second, when state and local officers encounter militant groups, it is imperative to know their ideology. There are militant political Muslims, and the American police should understand them, just as they study militant Christian and Jewish groups. Finally, understanding political Islam provides the background for conducting interviews and developing sources of information.

Future trends in terrorism indicate that the American police will face increased violence from religious terrorists. Many of these terrorists will be trained to meet law enforcement officers; they will be more thoroughly trained than any subjects police officers have encountered in the past. They will use technology to attack targets and information warfare to disrupt structures and services. Although policymakers have not settled on a role for state and local law enforcement in homeland defense, one factor is clear. America's enemies will bring the battle to police officers whether they have prepared for it or not.

References

Ahern, James F. (1972). *Police in Trouble*. New York: Hawthorne Books.

Al Qaeda. (n.d.). Al Qaeda Manual. Seized and translated by the Manchester Constabulary, United Kingdom.

American Civil Liberties Union. (3-20-02). "ACLU Decries Ashcroft Scheme to Gut Immigration Courts." (ONLINE). http://www.aclu.org/ACLUPressRelease

Armstrong, Karen. (2000). *Islam: A Short History*. New York: Random House.

Arquilla, John, David Ronfeldt, and Michele Zanini. (1999). "Networks, Netwar, and Information Age Terrorism," in Ian O. Lesser et al., eds., *Countering the New Terrorism*. Santa Monica, CA: RAND.

Baker, Al. (4-25-02). "At War College, Police Officials Will Work on Disaster Response." *New York Times*. (ONLINE). http://www.nytimes.com/2002/04/25/nyregion/25POLI.html

Barber, Benjamin R. (1996). *Jihad vs. McWorld: How Globalism and Tribalism are Reshaping the World*. New York: Ballantine Books.

Barkun, Michael. (1997). *Religion and the Racist Right: The Origins of the Christian Identity Movement*. Chapel Hill, NC: University of North Carolina Press.

Becker, Elizabeth. (7-14-02). "Brookings Study Calls Homeland Security Plans Too Ambitious." *New York Times*. (ONLINE). http://www.nytimes.com/2002/07/14/politics/14HOME.html

Bergen, Peter L. (2001). *Holy War, Inc.: Inside the Secret World of Osama bin Laden*. New York: The Free Press.

Berger, Peter L. (1980). *The Heretical Imperative: Contemporary Possibilities of Religious Affirmation*. Garden City, NY: Anchor Books.

Berlet, Chip. (1998). "Dances with Devils." (ONLINE). http://www.publiceye.org/Apocalyptic/Dances_with_Devils_2.htm

Best , Richard A., Jr. (12-3-01). *Intelligence and Law Enforcement: Countering Transnational Threats to the U.S.* CRS Report for Congress.

(ONLINE). http://www.fas.org/irp/crs/RL30252.pdf

Betts, Richard K. (2002). "Fixing Intelligence." *Foreign Affairs* (81): 43–59.

Biemer, John. (1-9-02). "In video, airline hijacker's traffic stop seen as routine." *Buffalo News*, A-6.

Blumberg, Abraham S. (1979). *Criminal Justice: Issues and Ironies*. New York: New Viewpoints.

Bodrero, D. Douglas. (2002). "Law Enforcement's New Challenge to Investigate, Interdict, and Prevent Terrorism." *The Police Chief* (February 2002): 41–48.

Bower, Amanda. (11-12-01). "Terrorist Hits and Misses: A Chronology of Mayhem." *Time*, 68.

Bruce, Steven. (1993). "Fundamentalism, Ethnicity, and Enclave." In Martin E. Marty and R. Scott Appleby, eds., *Fundamentalisms Observed*. Chicago: University of Chicago Press.

Byford, Grenville. (2002). "The Wrong War." *Foreign Affairs*, July/August (81): 34–43.

Calabresi, Massimo and Romesh Ratnesar. (3-11-02). "Can We Stop the Next Attack?" *Time*, 24–37.

California Department of Justice, Office of the Attorney General. (2002). Anti-Terrorist Information Center. (ONLINE). http://caag.state.ca.us/antiterrorism/index.htm

Cappel, Robert P. (1979). *S.W.A.T. Team Manual*. Boulder, CO: Paladin Press.

Center for Disease Control and Prevention. (2001). "Basic Facts about Anthrax." Atlanta: CDC.

Center for Disease Control and Prevention. (2001). "Basic Facts about Smallpox." Atlanta: CDC.

Chang, Nancy. (2001). "The USA Patriot Act: What's So Patriotic About Trampling on the Bill of Rights?" Center for Constitutional Rights. (ONLINE). http://www.ccr-ny.org/whatsnew/usa_patriot_act.asp

Christopher, William. (1999). "Report of the Independent Commission on the Los Angeles Police Department." In

Larry K. Gaines and Gary W. Cordner, eds., *Policing Perspectives: An Anthology*. Los Angeles: Roxbury.

Cilluffo, Frank J.; Sharon L. Cardash; and Gordon N. Lederman. (2001). *Combating Chemical, Biological, Radiological, and Nuclear Terrorism: A Comprehensive Strategy: A Report of the CSIS Homeland Defense Project*. Washington, DC: Center for Strategic and International Studies.

Clark, Richard. (2-13-02). Testimony on Cyberspace Security. United States Senate Subcommittee on the Judiciary. Washington, DC: United States Senate, recorded from C-Span.

Clausewitz, Carl von. (1984; orig. 1831). *On War*. Translated by Michael Howard and Peter Paret. Princeton, NJ: Princeton University Press.

Cloud, David S. (4-15-02). "Caught Off-Guard by Terror, the CIA Fights to Catch Up." *Wall Street Journal*, A1.

Clymer, Adam. (6-19-02). "Big Brother vs. Terrorist in Spy Camera Debate." *New York Times*. (ONLINE). http://www.nytimes.com/2002/06/19/national/19PRIV.html.

Colb, Sherry F. (10-10-01). "The New Face of Racial Profiling: How Terrorism Affects the Debate." *Find Law's Legal Commentary*. (ONLINE). http://writ.news.findlaw.com/200111 010.html

Commission on Accreditation for Law Enforcement Agencies. (1990). *Accreditation Program Overview*. Fairfax, VA: CALEA.

Commission on National Security. (2001). *United States Commission on National Security Report*. Washington, DC: Government Printing Office.

CONPLAN. (2001). *United States Government Interagency Domestic Terrorism Concept of Operations Plan*. Washington, DC: Government Printing Office.

Conti, Phillip M. (1977). *The Pennsylvania State Police*. New York: Stackpole.

Cooper, H. H. A., et al. (1976). *Report of the Task Force on Disorders and Terrorism*. Washington, DC: National Advisory

Committee on Criminal Justice Standards and Goals.

Craig, Gordon A. (1968). *The Politics of the Prussian Army: 1640–1945.* New York: Oxford University Press.

Critical Incident Analysis Group. (2001). *Threats to Symbols of American Democracy.* Charlottesville, VA: University of Virginia.

Crozier, Brian. (1975). "Terrorist Activity: International Terrorism." Hearings Before the Subcommittee to Investigate the Administration of the Internal Security Act and Other Internal Security Laws of the Committee on the Judiciary, 79th Congress, 1st session, Washington, DC: U.S. Senate.

Cummings, Jeanne. (8-13-02). "States Mend Homeland Security Blanket." *Wall Street Journal,* A4.

del Carmen, Rolando. (1991). *Civil Liberties in American Policing: A Text for Law Enforcement Personnel.* Englewood Cliffs, NJ: Prentice-Hall.

Department of Defense. (1-9-01). "DOD USS *Cole* Commission Report. (ONLINE). http://www.defenselink.mil/pubs/cole20010109.html

Dillon, Sam. (10-4-01). "A Forum Recalls Unheeded Warning." *New York Times,* A16.

Dobbs-Medras, Patricia (2002). *CFR-28.* Tallahassee, FL: Institute for Intergovernmental Research.

Downs, Anthony C. (1967). *Inside Bureaucracy.* Boston: Little, Brown.

Dreyfuss, Robert. (3-23-02). "The Cops are Watching You." (ONLINE). http://www.ccmep.org/hotnews2/cops_are_watching052302.htm

Dycus, Stephen. (7-26-02). "Be Careful About Calling in the Cavalry in the Struggle for Homeland Security." *Los Angeles Times.*

Dyson, William. (2002). *Overview of Terrorism.* Tallahassee, FL: Institute for Intergovernmental Research.

Electronic Frontier Foundation. (2001). "EEF Analysis of the Provisions of the USA Patriot Act." (ONLINE).

http://www.eef.org/Privacy/Surveillance/Terrorism_militias/20011031_eff_usa_Patriot_analysis.html

Elliot, Michael. (11-12-01). "The Hate Club." *Time,* 48–81.

Emerson, Steven. (2002). *American Jihad: The Terrorist Living Among Us.* New York: The Free Press.

Esposito, John. (1999). *The Islamic Threat: Myth or Reality,* 3rd ed. New York: Oxford University Press.

Farah, Caesar E. (2000). *Islam,* 6th ed. Hauppauge, NY: Baron's Educational.

Federal Bureau of Investigation. (2001). *An Introduction to Domestic Terrorism for State and Local Law Enforcement.* Quantico, VA: Federal Bureau of Investigation.

Fields, Gary. (5-3-02). "U.S. Probe of Intelligence Lapses to Go Beyond CIA and FBI." *Wall Street Journal,* A4.

Fineman, Mark and Stephen Braun. (9-24-01). "Life Inside al Qaeda: A Destructive Devotion." *Los Angeles Times.* (ONLINE). http://www.latimes.com/news/nationworld/world/la-092401alqaeda.story

Finn, Peter and Brooke A. Masters. (11-16-01). "Officials Seek Hijacker Who Wasn't: FBI Suspects Yemeni Man, Denied U.S. Visa, Is Missing Figure in September 11 Plot." *Washington Post,* A39.

Flynn, Stephen. (2002). "America the Vulnerable". *Foreign Affairs* (81): 60–74.

Fogelson, Robert M. (1977). *Big City Police.* Cambridge, MA: Harvard University Press.

Gaines, Larry K. and Gary W. Cordner. (1999). *Policing Perspectives: An Anthology.* Los Angeles: Roxbury.

Gibson, Scott Louis. (1974). "Theodore Roosevelt as President of the New York City Board of Police Commissioners." Master's Thesis, Michigan State University.

Goldstein, Herman. (1977). *Policing a Free Society.* Cambridge, MA: Ballinger.

Hanson, Victor Davis. (1989). *The Western Way of War: Infantry Battle in Ancient Greece*. New York: Alfred A. Knopf.

Harris, John W. (1987). "Domestic Terrorism in the 1980s." *FBI Law Enforcement Bulletin* (56): 5–13.

Herman, Susan. (12-3-01). "The USA Patriot Act and the U.S. Department of Justice: Losing our Balances". *Jurist*. (ONLINE). http://jurist.law.pitt.edu/forum/forumnew40.htm

Hinton, Henry L., Jr. (1999). *Combating Terrorism: Observations on Biological Terrorism and Public Health Initiatives*. Washington, DC: General Accounting Office.

Hitt, Greg and David S. Cloud. (6-10-02). "Bush's Homeland Security Overhaul Faces Obstacles." *Wall Street Journal*, A4.

Hoffman, Bruce. (1995). "Holy Terror: The Implications of Terrorism Motivated by a Religious Imperative." *Studies in Conflict and Terrorism* 18: 271–284.

Hoffman, Bruce. (1998). *Inside Terrorism*. New York: Columbia University Press.

Hoffman, Bruce. (1999). "Terrorism Trends and Prospects," in Ian O. Lesser, et al, eds., *Countering the New Terrorism*. Santa Monica, CA: RAND.

Hofstadter, Richard. (1965). *The Age of Reform: From Bryan to F.D.R.* New York: Knopf.

Holmes, J. J. (1971). "The National Guard of Pennsylvania: Policemen of Industry—1865–1905." Dissertation, University of Connecticut.

Howard, Michael. (1988). *Clausewitz*. New York: Oxford University Press.

Howard, Michael. (2002). "What's in a Name? How to Fight Terrorism." *Foreign Affairs* (81): 8–13.

Hudzik, John and Gary Cordner. (1983). *Planning in Criminal Justice Organizations and Systems*. New York: Macmillan.

Huntington, Samuel P. (1996). *The Clash of Civilizations and the Remaking of World Order*. New York: Simon and Schuster.

Institute for Global Education. (2001). "Panel Broadcast on the Middle East." Grand Rapids Public Access Television.

International Association of Chiefs of Police. (1967). *The Patrol Operation*. Alexandria, VA: IACP.

International Association of Chiefs of Police. (2001). *Terrorism Response*. Alexandria, VA: IACP.

Jacobs, Jeffrie. (1983). *S.W.A.T. Tactics*. Boulder, CO: Paladin Press.

Jenkins, Brian Michael. (1980). "Nuclear Terrorism and Its Consequences." *Society* (July/August): 5–16.

Jenkins, Brian Michael. (1983). *New Modes of Conflict*. Santa Monica, CA: RAND.

Jenkins, Brian Michael. (1986). "Is Nuclear Terrorism Plausible?" In Paul Leventhal and Yonah Alexander eds., *Nuclear Terrorism*. New York: Pergamon.

Jenkins, Brian Michael. (1987). "Will Terrorists Go Nuclear?" In Walter Laqueur and Yonah Alexander eds., *The Terrorism Reader*. New York: Meridian.

Johnson, D. R. (1981). *American Law Enforcement: A History*. St. Louis, MO: Forum.

Johnson, Kevin. (1-29-02). "NYPD adds CIA, military experts." *USA Today*. (ONLINE). http://www.usatoday.com/news/nation/2002/01/29/usat-new-york.htm

Juergensmeyer, Mark. (2000). *Terror in the Mind of God: The Global Rise of Religious Violence*. Berkeley, CA: University of California Press.

Katz, Charles M. (2001). "The Establishment of a Police Gang Unit: An Examination of Organizational and Environmental Factors." *Criminology* (39): 37–73.

Katz, Lewis R. (11-24-01). "Anti-Terrorism Laws: Too Much of a Good Thing." *Jurist* (ONLINE). http://jurist.law.pitt.edu/forum/forumnew39.htm

Kayyem, Juliette and Arnold M. Howitt (eds.). (2002). *Beyond the Beltway: Focusing on Hometown Security*. Cambridge, MA: A Report of the

Executive Session on Domestic Preparedness, John F. Kennedy School of Government, Harvard University.

Keathley, James. (2002). *Undercover Operations in Domestic Terrorism.* Tallahassee, FL: Institute for Intergovernmental Research.

Kelsay, John. (1993). *Islam and War.* Louisville, KY: John Knox Press.

Kepel, Gilles. (2001). *Jihad: The Trail of Political Islam.* Cambridge, MA: Belknap Harvard University Press.

Kolko, Gabriel. (1963). *The Triumph of Conservatism: A Reinterpretation of American History, 1900–1916.* New York: Free Press.

Konotorovich, E. V. (6-18-02). "Make Them Talk." *Wall Street Journal,* A12.

Kraska, Peter and Victor Kappeler. (1999). "Militarizing American Police: The Rise and Normalization of Paramilitary Units." In Larry K. Gaines and Gary W. Cordner, eds., *Policing Perspectives: An Anthology.* Los Angeles: Roxbury.

Kraska, Peter B. (1996). "Enjoying Militarism: Political/Personal Dilemmas in Studying U.S. Police Paramilitary Units." *Justice Quarterly* (13): 405–429.

Lane, Roger. (1975). *Policing the City: Boston—1822–1885.* New York: Antheneum.

Laqueur, Walter. (1999). *The New Terrorism: Fanaticism and the Arms of Mass Destruction.* New York: Oxford University Press.

Law Enforcement News. (10-15-01). "Secret weapon against terrorism?" John Jay College of Criminal Justice. (ONLINE). http://www.lib.jjay.cuny.edu/len/2001/10.15/html

Lesser, Ian O., Bruce Hoffman, John Arquilla, David Ronfeldt; Michele Zanini; and Brian Michael Jenkins. (1999). *Countering the New Terrorism.* Santa Monica, CA: RAND.

Levitt, Leonard. (1-28-02). "A Fed-Friendly NYPD? Not Yet." *News Day.* (ONLINE). http://newsday.com/news/columnists/ny-nyplaz22256708jan28.column

Lichtblau, Eric. (9-29-01). "Impassioned Letter Left Behind by Hijackers Urges Them to Stay the Course in Return for Paradise." *Los Angeles Times.* (ONLINE). http://www.latimes.com/news/nationworld/nation/la-092901letter.story

Liddell Hart, Basil H. (1967). *Strategy.* New York: Praeger.

Lindsay, James M. and Audrey Singer. (5-8-02). "Local Police Should Not Do a Federal Job." *New York Times.* (ONLINE). http://nytimes.com/2002/05/08/opinion/08SING.html

Liptak, Adam. (5-31-02). "Changing the Standard." *New York Times.* (ONLINE). http://nytimes.com/2002/05/31/national/31ASSE.html

Management Analytics and Others. (1995). Sun Tzu: The Art of War. http://www.all.net.books/tzu/html

Manning, Peter K. (1977). *Police Work: The Social Organization of Policing.* Cambridge, MA: Massachusetts Institute of Technology.

Masters, Brooke A. (11-30-01). "Prosecutors Link Virginia Man To Third September 11 Hijacker: Terrorist Used His Arlington Address on Visa Application." *Wall Street Journal* A14.

Mattoon, Steven. (1987). *S.W.A.T. Training and Deployment.* Boulder, CO: Paladin Press.

McConnell, Grant C. (1970). *Private Power and American Democracy.* New York: Vintage.

Miller, Judith, Stephen Engelberg, and William Broad. (2001). *Germs: Biological Weapons and America's Secret War.* New York: Simon and Schuster.

Mitchell, Alison, and Carl Hulse. (6-27-02). "Accountability Concern Is Raised Over Security Department." *The New York Times.* (ONLINE). http://www.nytimes.com/2002/06/27/national/27RIDG.html

National Drug Intelligence Center. (2002). "Working for a Safer

America." Johnstown, PA: Department of Justice.

National Public Radio. (12-6-01). "Liberty vs. Security: An NPR Special Report." (ONLINE). http://www.npr.org/programs/specials/liberties/index.html

New Jersey State Police. (2002). Intelligence Service Section. (ONLINE). http://www.state.nj.us/lps/njsp/about/intel.html

New York Times on the Web. (11-27-01). "More than 550 held on terrorist suspicion." http://nytimes.com, nvestigation.html

Nilson, Chad and Tod Burke. (2002). "Environmental Extremists and the Eco-Terrorism Movement." *ACJS Today* (24): 1–6.

Nordland, Rod; Sami Yousafzi; and Babak Dehghanpisheh. (8-19-02). "How al Qaeda Slipped Away." *Newsweek*, 34–41.

Office of Homeland Security. (2002). *National Strategy for Homeland Security.* Washington, DC: Office of Homeland Security.

Organization for the Prohibition of Chemical Weapons. (2000). "Nerve Agents: Lethal Organo-Phosphorus Compounds Inhibiting Cholinesterase." (ONLINE). http://www.opcw.nl/chemhaz/nerve.htm

Osterholm, Michael T. and John Schwartz. (2000). *Living Terrors.* New York: Delta.

Parker, Laura. (1-23-02). "A Frenzied Race for Answers, Antibiotics." *USA Today,* 6A.

PBS. (2001a). "Looking for Answers." *Frontline*, PBS Video: FROL 2000.

PBS. (2001b). "Target America." *Frontline,* PBS Video: 2003.

Pennsylvania Federation of Labor. (1915). *American Cossack.* Harrisburg, PA: PSFL.

Perl, Raphael F. (1998). *Terrorism: U.S. Response to Bombings in Kenya and Tanzania: A New Policy Direction?* CRS Report for Congress: (ONLINE) http://usinfo.state.gov/topical/pol/terror/crs96091.htm

Perl, Raphael F. (2001). *National Commission on Terrorism: Background and Issues for Congress.* February 6. (ONLINE) http://www.maurizioturco.it/National_Security_Achive/Terrorism_and_US_ Policy/crs20010206.pdf

Police: The Law Enforcement Magazine. (July 2002). "Survey." (ONLINE). http://policemag.com/t_homt.cfm

Radelet, Louis and David Carter. (2000). *Police and the Community,* 7th ed. New York: Macmillan.

Ranstorp, Magnus. (1998). "Interpreting the Broader Context and Meaning of bin Ladin's Fatwa." *Studies in Conflict and Terrorism,* 21: 321–330.

Reppetto, Thomas A. (1978). *The Blue Parade.* New York: Free Press.

Riordan, Richard J. and Amy B. Zegart. (7-5-02). "City Hall Goes to War." *New York Times.* (ONLINE). http://www.nytimes.com/2002/07/05/opinion/05RIOR.html

Rosenbaum, David E. (6-19-02). "Bush Allies Direct Fire Against FBI and CIA." *New York Times.* (ONLINE). http://www.nytimes.com/2002/06/19/politics/19SENA.html

Ross, Jeffery Ian. (1999). "Beyond the Conceptualization of Terrorism: A Psychological-Structural Model of the Causes of This Activity." In Craig Summers and Eric Markusen eds., *Collective Violence: Harmful Behavior in Groups and Governments.* New York: Rowen and Littlefield.

Rotunda, R. D. (1987). *Constitutional Law.* St. Paul, MN: West Publishing.

Schmitt, Eric. (4-29-02). "Administration Split on Local Role in Terror Fight." *New York Times.* (ONLINE). http://www.nytimes.com/2002/04/29/politics/29IMMI.html

Schoof, Mark and Gary Fields. (3-25-02). "Anthrax Attack Summary." *Wall Street Journal,* A20.

Seelye, Katherine Q. (6-23-02). "War on Terror Makes for Odd Twists in Justice System." *New York Times.* (ONLINE).

http://www.nytimes.com/2002/06/29/national/23SUSP.html

Shay, Saul. (2002). *The Endless Jihad: The Mujahidin, the Taliban, and bin Laden.* Herzliya, Israel: Institute for Counterterrorism.

Shenon, Philip and David Stout. (5-21-02). "Rumsfeld Says Terrorists Will Use Weapons of Mass Destruction." *New York Times.* (ONLINE). http://www.nytimes.com/2002/05/21/politics/CND-TERROR/html

Shenon, Philip. (5-21-02). "Suicide Attacks Certain in U.S., Mueller Warns." *New York Times* (ONLINE). http://www.nytimes.com/2002/05/21/national/21terror.html

Sherman, Lawrence W. (1978). *The Quality of Police Education.* San Francisco: Josey-Bass.

Stinson, James. (2002). "Al Qaeda." Mid-Atlantic Great Lakes Organized Crime Law Enforcement Network Conference. Cleveland, Ohio. April 25, 2002.

Straub, Noelle. (5-1-02). "USA Patriot Act Power Prompt Second Look." *The Hill.* (ONLINE). http://www.thehil.com/050102/patriot.shtm

Sulc, Lawrence B. (1996). *Law Enforcement Counter Intelligence.* Shawnee Mission, KS: Varno Press.

Swanson, Charles R., Leonard Territo, and Robert W. Taylor. (2001). *Police Administration: Structures, Processes, and Behavior,* 5th ed. Upper Saddle River, NJ: Prentice-Hall.

Taylor, Robert W. (1987). "Terrorism and Intelligence." *Defense Analysis* (3): 165–175.

Taylor, Robert W. (2002). *Understanding Terrorism in the Middle East.* Tallahassee, FL: Institute for Intergovernmental Research.

The Economist. (12-22-01). "Homeland Security."

Thornburgh, Dick. (6-29-02). "Well Before September 11, Congress Overtaxed the FBI." *New York Times.* (ONLINE). http://www.

nytimes.com/2002/06/29/opinion/29THOR.html

Tyler, Patrick E. and Neil MacFarquhar. (6-4-02). "Egypt Warned U.S. of al Qaeda Plot, Mubarak Asserts." *New York Times.* (ONLINE). http://nytimes.com/2002/06/04/national04WARN.html

United States Congress, Office of Technology Assessment. (1995). *Environmental Monitoring for Nuclear Safeguards.* Washington, DC: Government Printing Office.

United States General Accounting Office, National Security and International Affairs Division. (1999). *Combating Terrorism: Analysis of Emergency Response Equipment and Sustainment Costs.* Washington, DC: General Accounting Office.

United States of America v. Mohamad Youssef Hammoud, et al. (March 2002). United States District Court, Western District of North Carolina, Charlotte Division. Docket No. 3:00CR147-MU.

Valburn, Marjorie. (2-4-02). "Air Marshal Program Drains Other Agencies." *Wall Street Journal,* A18.

Van Creveld, Martin. (1985). *Command in War.* Cambridge, MA: Harvard University Press.

Van Natta, Don, Jr. (3-30-02). "Government Will Ease Limits on Domestic Spying." *New York Times.* (ONLINE). http://www.nytimes.com/2002/03/30.html

Varadarajan, Tunku. (5-3-02). "How Muslims Live Now." *Wall Street Journal.*

Vatis, Michael A. (1999). *Emergency Law Enforcement Services Vulnerability Survey.* Quantico, VA: Federal Bureau of Investigation.

Vatis, Michael A. (2001). *Cyber Attacks During the War on Terrorism: A Predictive Analysis.* Hanover, NH: Institute for Security Technology Studies, Dartmouth College.

Walker, Samuel. (1975). "Urban Police in American History." *Journal of Police Science and Administration* (3): 336–345.

Walker, Samuel. (1977). *A Critical History of Police Reform: The Emergence of Professionalism*. Lexington, MA: D.C. Heath.

Walker, Samuel. (1985). *Sense and Nonsense about Crime: A Policy Guide*. Pacific Grove, CA: Brooks/Cole.

Walker, Samuel. (1992). *The Police in America*. New York: McGraw Hill.

Wardlaw, Grant. (1982). *Political Terrorism: Theory, Tactics, and Counter-Measures*. London: Cambridge University Press.

Warwick, Donald P. (1975). *A Theory of Public Bureaucracy: Politics, Personality, and Organization in the State Department*. Cambridge, MA: Harvard University Press.

Washington Post. (11-20-01). "Northern Virginia Man Charged in Fraud Case." A12.

Watson, Dale L. (2002). *The Terrorist Threat Confronting the United States*. Washington, DC: Federal Bureau of Investigation, www.fbi.gov.

Weber, Max. (1947). *The Theory of Social and Economic Organization*. New Free Press, 1947.

Wedgwood, Ruth. (6-14-02). "The Enemy Within." *Wall Street Journal*, A12.

Weinstein, James. (1968). *The Corporate Ideal in the Liberal State—1900–1918*. Boston: Beacon.

Weiss, Rick. (10-18-01). "Clarifying the Facts and Risks of Anthrax." *Washington Post*. (ONLINE). http://www.washingtonpost.com/ac2/wp-dyn/A12043-2001Oct17?

White, Jonathan R. (2003). *Terrorism: An Introduction*. Belmont, CA: Wadsworth.

Wilgoren, Jodi. (6-19-02). "At One of 1,000 Front Lines in U.S., Local Officials Try to Plan for War." *New York Times*. (ONLINE). http://www.nytimes.com/2002/06/19/national/19HOME.html

Wilkinson, Paul. (1974). *Political Terrorism*. New York: Wiley.

Wilkinson, Paul. (1986). "Trends in International Terrorism and the American Response." In Lawrence Freeman *et al* eds., *Terrorism and International Order*. London: Routledge & Kegan Paul.

Wilkinson, Paul. (1994). *Terrorism: British Perspectives*. New York: Hall.

Wise, David. (6-2-02). "Spy Game: Changing the Rules So the Good Guys Win." *New York Times*. (ONLINE). http://www.nytimes.com/2002/06/02/weekinreview/02WISEhtml

Woolsey, James. (7-29-02). "The Coming Revolution in Iran." *Wall Street Journal*, A14.

Wright, Robin. (1986). *Sacred Rage*. New York: Touchstone.

Wright, Robin. (1989). *In the Name of God: The Khomeini Decade*. New York: Praeger.

Young, John A. T. and R. John Collier. (2002). "Attacking Anthrax." *Scientific American* (March): 48–59.

Index